The Day Trading Lies

The Ugly Truth Behind Day Trading's Shiny Promises

By Cornelius Nathaniel Goldman

Table of Contents

Prologue

You've seen the ads, the promises of luxury, freedom, and wealth just one trade away. They show you the young guy in a sports car, the woman sipping drinks on a beach, whispering, "This could be you." But behind every polished post, there's another story—of empty bank accounts, sleepless nights, and shattered lives. They don't show you the faces of those staring at their screens at 3 a.m., hands shaking, wondering where it all went wrong.

Maybe you've felt the thrill of a lucky trade, the rush of money gained. But have you felt the crash? The gut-wrenching loss that follows, the urge to "win it back" as your life unravels before you? Day trading promises freedom, but often it's a trap. It takes your time, your money, your peace, and sometimes your very sanity.

This book won't sell you dreams. It's here to tear away the lies, to show you the truth behind the hype and the glamour. Before you take the plunge, turn the page. Find out what day trading really costs, and ask yourself if you're willing to pay the price.

Most of the stories shared in this book are real-life cases, though names have been changed out of respect for the individuals involved.

Chapter 1:

The Illusion of Easy Wealth

1. The Hook: "Get Rich Quick" Seduction

A young man named Alex, overwhelmed with financial stress, discovers a YouTube video that promises to reveal how "day trading can transform your life in just a few months."

In his nightly search for financial answers, Alex finds videos and social media posts showcasing people his age seemingly living a luxury lifestyle with minimal effort. The message is clear: if they can do it, so can he.

Alex becomes captivated, scrolling late into the night, increasingly convinced that he's stumbled upon the "shortcut" to financial freedom.

This example can emphasize the emotional vulnerability that marketing often exploits, especially for people in financial difficulty, job dissatisfaction, or seeking a way out of a 9-to-5 lifestyle.

2. The "Instant Success" Sales Pitch

Illustration the promises that saturate day trading marketing:

      o "Make six figures in six months!"

      o "Leave your 9-to-5 and live off your day trading profits."

o "Minimal investment needed! Start with as little as $100 and change your life."

- These claims are carefully constructed to make day trading seem universally accessible, suggesting that anyone can achieve success regardless of background or expertise.

- Some or Many Bestselling day trading books and social media ads, phrases and imagery promise an "insider" look at financial success. These strategies are designed to create a sense of exclusivity, as though readers are just one step away from joining an elite club.

3. Social Media's Role in the Illusion

How social media platforms like Instagram, YouTube, and TikTok create a high-pressure environment:

Influencers use photos of luxury items—sports cars, yachts, designer clothes—to imply that day trading alone funds their lifestyles. Its all staged and not only do many do this but also either do not expose other but also help each other out in collaboration videos or settings/ investments and so on.

The theme of "flexing" wealth in videos, where creators film themselves in lavish surroundings or traveling, using captions like "All thanks to day trading." These presentations reinforce the idea that day trading is a fast track to riches, making viewers feel as if they're missing out on a hidden opportunity.

Buying Influencers:

Many of the most successful "fakes" hire influencers to show off lifestyles or participate in financial collaborations. Constant exposure to these curated images can lead viewers to feel inadequate or "behind," creating a false sense of urgency to take action. This urgency is often a manufactured psychological tactic that influencers exploit, pressuring followers to jump into trading immediately.

4. Selective Success Stories: The "Winner's Circle" Illusion

Only the most successful (and often rare) cases of high profits are highlighted in day trading communities.

Casino: people only hear about the jackpot winners, never the countless others who lose money. This selective sharing creates a "winner's circle" illusion, where people assume that success in day trading is common.

In reality, studies have shown a vast majority of day traders lose money, especially within the first few months. Influencers and "gurus" avoid discussing this, instead crafting an environment where failure is stigmatized or blamed on the trader's lack of commitment.

This illusion pressures individuals to keep going, thinking they're "almost there" when, in fact, they're trapped in a cycle of losses. The shame around failure keeps many silent, reinforcing the illusion that day trading is a near-certain path to wealth.

5. FOMO: The "Act Now" Pressure Tactic

How marketers create FOMO (Fear of Missing Out), implying that day trading is a fleeting opportunity that requires immediate action.

Examples : "Get in now before the market changes!" or "Only a few know this secret; don't miss out on your chance!"

Influencers and financial "gurus" often use limited-time offers, countdowns, and phrases like "only a few spots left" to create a sense of urgency. This tactic pressures people to act without fully researching the risks.

Psychological impact of FOMO, especially when followers see friends or peers investing. The "fear of missing out" is amplified when individuals feel as though they're the last ones to seize an "opportunity" others are already profiting from.

FOMO not only clouds judgment but also drives people into impulsive decisions that can lead to devastating financial outcomes.

6. Hiding the Complexity of Day Trading

The vast majority of day trading promotions ignore or significantly downplay the skills, experience, and deep market knowledge required to succeed.

The reality of day trading's complexity: to trade effectively, one must understand technical indicators, chart patterns, risk management, economic trends, and market psychology.

Comparing day trading to professions that require formal training—yet many advertisements make it seem as if day trading can be mastered with a few YouTube videos and "insider secrets."

Revealing that most day traders spend months or years practicing with no guarantee of success, and that significant, consistent profits typically require full-time dedication and a thorough understanding of the markets—elements that influencers and marketers conveniently gloss over.

7. The Emotional Highs and Lows of Day Trading

The psychological highs associated with early wins and the addictive nature of "chasing the high."

- o Initial successes create a rush, leading many to invest more in hopes of multiplying their profits.
- o Contrasting this with the extreme lows that follow losses, where people may feel guilt, shame, or self-doubt, especially when they've invested money they couldn't afford to lose.

The emotional roller coaster that ensnares traders in an endless cycle of highs (wins) and lows (losses). Each win renews hope, while each loss fuels desperation, creating a pattern that's hard to break.

Influencers rarely mention these emotional pitfalls, painting day trading as consistently positive while hiding the toll it takes on one's mental and emotional health.

Chapter 2:

The True Costs of Starting Out

1. Opening Story: The False Hope of a "Small Investment"

Example: Sarah in more detail: a 28-year-old administrative assistant, dealing with daily financial pressures—student loans, car payments, and saving up for her first apartment.

Sarah's initial excitement to start day trading is sparked by social media ads promising that "anyone can become a day trader," with just $100 to get started. She reasons that $500 isn't much to invest if it could help her build wealth and pay off debts sooner.

She quickly realizes, however, that her account balance doesn't hold up against even minor fees. Over a few weeks, Sarah finds herself frustrated and demoralized as each trade chips away at her small account balance.

As Sarah contemplates adding more money, she feels the pressure mounting—an early hint of the "sunk cost" effect that many beginners face. She's emotionally invested and financially strained, yet the hope of "big returns" keeps her pushing forward.

2. The Myth of the "Small Investment"

Exploring the widespread but misleading idea that day trading is accessible to anyone, regardless of initial capital.

- o Many advertisements push the message that trading is an equal-opportunity field. However, starting with $100 or $200 only covers a few trades before fees and small losses take a toll.

Illustration with precise math:

Consider the typical trade fee of $5. On a $100 trade, this fee represents a 5% reduction in the account balance immediately—making it difficult to profit enough to cover just the cost of trading.

Walk through a scenario where a $100 trade nets a 1% gain. After fees, this leaves a minuscule profit or even a loss, underscoring how limited capital gets depleted quickly.

- Many traders find they need at least $2,000 to $5,000 to start with any semblance of security, allowing for both strategic losses and occasional fees. Even then, profits are often minimal at first.

3. The Necessity of "Disposable Income"

Defining disposable income and explaining why advisors recommend only using money one can afford to lose.

For most people, disposable income is limited. It's what's left after rent, bills, groceries, loan payments, and essential savings. Often, the "leftover" amount is reserved for emergencies, not speculative trading.

Example Calculation:

If someone earns $3,000 per month, with essential expenses consuming $2,500, they may only have $500 left as "disposable income." Investing this in day trading means risking their entire discretionary fund for the month.

- o If they lose this money, they face a tight month financially, risking stress or debt.

- Emphasizing that without a cushion, beginners are forced to take greater risks, trading out of necessity rather than strategy, which often leads to poor decisions and amplifies losses.

4. The True Cost of Learning and Practicing

Breaking down the practical costs that newcomers face when trying to learn day trading, including:

Courses and Mentorships:

Many "gurus" sell beginner courses that appear necessary but often only scratch the surface of what's truly required for success.

Prices range from $500 for entry-level courses to $3,000 or more for advanced mentorship programs. However, these courses often end up being sales funnels for even pricier "exclusive" mentorships.

Software and Subscriptions:

Highlighting that while many platforms offer free demos, serious trading requires advanced tools for analysis and real-time data feeds.

Monthly subscriptions can range from $50 to over $200 for high-quality software, charting tools, and premium data. For someone starting with a $1,000 account, these fees can eat up their funds quickly.

Real-Life Practice and Live Trading:

Many traders start with demo accounts, thinking it's a way to practice without risk. However, live trading adds psychological pressure that demo accounts can't simulate, often pushing beginners to trade more recklessly or take higher risks when their own money is on the line.

Realizing this difference often drives beginners to spend even more, seeking out "advanced" courses or tools that they believe will help bridge the gap.

Example Scenario: Suppose a beginner spends $1,500 on an initial course, $100/month on software, and $50/month on data. In a year, they will have spent over $2,500, not including any funds for actual trading. This overhead adds up quickly and often becomes a financial burden.

5. The Opportunity Cost of Day Trading

Introducing the concept of opportunity cost—time and resources spent on day trading that could have been invested elsewhere.

Example of Time Investment:

Beginners often dedicate 15–20 hours a week to learning, researching, and practicing trades. This commitment takes time away from work, family, hobbies, and even potential side jobs that would provide guaranteed income.

For someone working a minimum-wage job, 15 hours could mean $150 a week in extra income, or $600 a month. In contrast, a beginner day trader may spend this time only to break even or face losses.

Missed Income from Stable Investments:

Compare day trading with traditional investment methods like index funds or retirement accounts, which can yield steady returns with far less time and risk.

Time spent learning day trading often yields minimal returns, whereas the same time spent in traditional investments could provide long-term growth without the volatility.

- Opportunity cost reveals that day trading's "cost" isn't just financial—it's the forfeited potential for stability and guaranteed income from other sources.

- Consider for example how many hours most people spend watching free info or instruction videos about any topics, and the time they spend comparing the information and verifying if its true.

- How many hours have you spend/ wasted watching "people who know" or experts and at the end knowing it was a total waste of your time?

6. The Debt Trap: Funding Trading Accounts with Loans

The lure of quick profits can lead people to take on debt to fund their day trading, believing they'll "earn it back" with profits.

Example of the Debt Spiral:

A beginner takes out a $2,000 personal loan at 15% interest. They invest the full amount in a trading account but lose half within weeks.

Now, they not only owe $2,000 but also must pay interest on funds that were lost to trading. They feel pressured to take even higher risks to "win back" the lost money, often resulting in further losses.

- Many people fall into the debt trap, relying on credit cards, payday loans, or cash advances to keep trading after initial losses. This creates a vicious cycle where debt accumulates alongside trading losses, worsening their financial situation.

- **Debt-driven trading** adds immense psychological strain, as the pressure to recover losses fuels impulsive trading, leading to further debt and financial stress.

- **Always avoid Debt-Driven Trading!!!**

7. The Emotional Toll of Starting with Limited Funds

Psychological impact of trading with small amounts. Each loss is magnified, making beginners feel that every trade is a make-or-break decision.

Example of Psychological Strain:

Sarah's experience trading with $500. Every $5 fee, every small loss, feels like a hit to her confidence. The pressure leads her to avoid trades she believes are "too risky," and soon she feels defeated, as her funds barely make any returns.

When small profits fail to cover previous losses, frustration and anxiety set in. Instead of excitement, Sarah feels trapped, constantly second-guessing every move.

- Many traders in this position find themselves "chasing" losses—doubling down on risky trades in hopes of recovering small losses, leading to even bigger setbacks.

- The psychological stress of watching an account drain slowly can erode confidence, push traders to make irrational decisions, and ultimately make trading unsustainable for those without significant capital.

8. The Misleading Nature of Influencer Marketing

Influencers and gurus exploit the aspirational appeal of day trading, often promoting it as a path anyone can pursue without clarifying the true costs involved.

- Influencers typically display only success stories, avoiding mention of the expenses and emotional pressures that newcomers face.

- Many influencers aren't day traders themselves; they profit from selling courses, affiliate marketing, or partnerships with trading platforms, benefiting from followers' losses.

- Some influencers collaborate with unscrupulous individuals for a quick payout, fully aware they might—or almost certainly will—lose their accounts and followers. However, the large sum they receive often compensates for a few, or even many, years of work.

Case in Point:

Many influencers display large profits from trading but fail to mention that these profits come from years of experience or large trading accounts, far beyond the reach of an average beginner.

- This marketing creates unrealistic expectations, leading followers to underestimate the real costs and risks of starting out, and to ignore signs that day trading isn't suited for everyone.

Conclusion: Laying the Foundation for Realistic Expectations

Day trading's "small investment" myth is a misleading concept that hides the extensive financial and emotional costs.

Only those with disposable income, a tolerance for risk, and the readiness to absorb both financial and time-related opportunity costs should consider day trading.

Influencers especially without the technical knowledge should not be just blindly believed and followed.

Debt-Driven trading is only for the rich or experts do not try it, not even for a small amount. Furthermore, many ore most end up paying more than they made.

Chapter 3:

The Misleading Math of Small Trades

1. Opening Story: The Illusion of Small, Consistent Profits

Example: Mark in more detail: a 29-year-old teacher looking for a side income. After seeing advertisements and social media posts from influencers, he's convinced that he can grow his money gradually by making small, frequent trades. These influencers often promise that "even a few dollars per trade can add up to substantial wealth."

Mark deposits $500 and plans to make several small trades daily, hoping to make incremental gains that he believes will add up over time.

After a few weeks, he begins to notice that each time he makes a small profit, a large portion is eaten up by fees and spreads. Despite his best efforts, his account balance is barely increasing—sometimes even decreasing. This story serves as a relatable example of the disillusionment many beginners feel after realizing the reality of small trades.

2. The Concept of Scalping and Small Profit Margins

The concept of "scalping," a common day trading strategy promoted to beginners, where traders aim for quick profits by making numerous small trades throughout the day.

Scalping is frequently marketed as an easy path to steady returns, with the promise that "small profits add up" if done consistently.

- However, this strategy is highly challenging to execute profitably due to hidden costs and high risks.

For every trade, scalpers need to ensure their profits exceed not only fees but also potential losses from a single unsuccessful trade.

Example Calculation:

Mark attempts to make a 1% profit on each $100 trade, or $1 per trade. But after factoring in a $2 fee per trade, he finds that each successful trade results in a net loss.

Over time, he realizes that it takes multiple successful trades just to break even due to the high impact of fees.

3. The High Cost of Fees and Commissions

Break down the significant impact of trading fees and commissions on small trades, which many beginners overlook.

Types of Fees:

Commission Fees: Most trading platforms charge a fee per trade, typically between $1 and $10, which can be a huge cost relative to small trade profits.

Spread Costs: The spread is the difference between the buy and sell price, which can lead to immediate losses if the price shifts during the trade.

Hidden Fees: Many brokers add extra fees for advanced tools, premium data, or even inactivity, further eroding small profits.

Detailed Example with Fees and Commissions:

Suppose Mark makes twenty $100 trades, each with a goal of 1% profit ($1 per trade). His gross earnings would be $20. But with a $2 fee per trade, his total fees add up to $40, meaning he's actually lost $20 overall, even with a high percentage of successful trades.

These costs add up quickly, forcing beginner traders to work just to cover fees and avoid net losses, which can be a disheartening and financially draining experience.

4. Spread Costs: The Invisible Losses of Small Trades

The concept of "spread," represents the difference between the buy price and sell price of a stock or asset. In day trading, spreads can be highly volatile, causing unintended losses even on successful trades.

Example:

Mark buys a stock at $10.00 with a goal of selling it at $10.10 for a small profit. However, due to a slight shift in the spread, he ends up selling at $9.98, creating a small but impactful loss.

Over time, these small fluctuations add up, creating a hidden cost that scalpers often overlook when they aim for quick trades with minimal profit margins.

- Illustrates how spread costs alone can prevent consistent profits and force traders to win at a much higher rate to offset these hidden losses.

5. Compound Growth: Why the Math Doesn't Add Up for Small Trades

Influencers often promote the concept of compound growth, suggesting that small, regular gains can "snowball" into substantial wealth over time.

The Reality of Interrupted Compounding:

While compound growth can work for long-term investments, day trading profits rarely grow exponentially because of constant interruptions from losses, fees, and taxes.

Example Calculation:

If Mark hypothetically earns a 1% profit daily, his account should double in 70 trading days if no losses, fees, or taxes occur. However, due to inevitable interruptions, this is unrealistic.

- Each time Mark incurs a fee, a loss, or a tax, the compounding cycle is broken, preventing the steady growth needed for exponential gains.

The Psychological Impact:

Beginners often become frustrated and confused when they fail to see the compounding effect they've been promised, leading to discouragement and doubt in their trading abilities.

6. How Losses Quickly Wipe Out Small Gains

The role of losses in diminishing profits, especially in day trading, where small trades are vulnerable to even minor setbacks.

Calculation of Losses vs. Gains:

If Mark makes five successful trades with a 2% profit each, he has a total gain of 10%. However, a single 5% loss erases half of his profits.

This cycle of small wins and occasional losses means traders are constantly working to recover rather than grow their accounts, creating a situation where progress is painstakingly slow or nonexistent.

- Highlights the emotional toll of this cycle: Many traders experience the "one step forward, two steps back" feeling, as gains are frequently offset by minor but inevitable losses. This often leads to frustration, burnout, and risky decision-making in an attempt to break even.

7. The Impact of Taxes on Small Gains

Taxes further erode the minimal profits that day traders make, especially in countries where short-term capital gains are taxed at higher rates.

Short-Term Capital Gains Tax:

In the U.S., day trading profits are taxed as short-term capital gains, with rates equivalent to regular income tax (often between 20-37% depending on income level).

Detailed Example Calculation:

If Mark makes $1,000 in day trading profits over a year and his tax rate is 25%, he owes $250 in taxes. After fees and taxes, his actual profit is significantly lower than anticipated.

The tax burden can be devastating for beginners who don't account for taxes, resulting in net losses even after "successful" trading periods.

- While influencers often display gross profits, they rarely discuss the impact of taxes on actual, take-home profits, leaving beginners with a distorted view of what day trading actually yields.

8. The Temptation to Scale Up: The Trap of High-Risk Trades

Many traders, frustrated by minimal returns from small trades, feel pressured to "scale up" by risking larger amounts on individual trades.

Example of Scaling Up:

Mark, disappointed by his $1-$2 profits per trade, decides to risk $500 on a single trade to achieve a more substantial profit. One 10% loss on this trade means he loses $50, a setback that erases weeks of small gains.

This need to scale up exposes beginners to more significant losses. Scaling up, while seemingly the only option, often leads to poor decision-making under emotional pressure, further compounding losses.

- Highlighting that scaling up too early is a common beginner mistake, as the emotional stakes rise with higher amounts, making trades more stressful and risky.

9. The Influence of Success Stories and Unrealistic Expectations

Influencers often showcase success stories where they or someone else turned a small account into a large one. These stories set up unrealistic expectations for beginners.

Many of these success stories either involve unusually favorable market conditions, experienced traders, or simply luck—factors not replicable by most beginners.

Example: An influencer shows a screenshot of their account growing from $1,000 to $10,000 in a month, without explaining that they used high-risk trades, borrowed money, or simply benefitted from a rare market upswing.

- Emphasizing: beginners often internalize these stories, setting unrealistic goals for themselves and feeling inadequate when their own results don't match up. This can lead to over-trading, chasing losses, or falling for paid "secrets" that promise similar outcomes.

10. The Emotional and Psychological Toll of Small, Eroded Gains

The emotional toll of seeing minimal profits after investing significant time, energy, and money into day trading.

Many traders find themselves exhausted, frustrated, and demoralized when their hard work yields small, inconsistent returns that are quickly eaten up by fees and losses.

Example of Emotional Impact:

Mark, after several months, finds himself questioning his abilities and wondering if he's "not cut out" for trading. The disappointment leads to a sense of failure and doubt, causing him to either take bigger risks or consider quitting entirely.

- Constant stress of chasing small, eroded gains leads to burnout, poor decision-making, and impulsive trading. Many traders, disillusioned with their minimal returns, feel trapped in a cycle of "trying to make it work" despite minimal progress.

Closing: The Reality Check on Small Trades

Reinforcing the reality that small, frequent trades are often unprofitable due to hidden costs, fees, taxes, and market volatility.

Emphasizing that while influencers make it seem like small trades can generate steady income, they rarely work for beginners with limited capital due to the compounding impact of costs.

Chapter 4:

The Fake Positivity Trap

1. Opening Story: The Pull of Positive Messaging and Success Stories

Example: Jenna, a 25-year-old marketing assistant who feels limited in her financial prospects and dreams of a more prosperous future. She stumbles upon the world of day trading through social media influencers, where positivity reigns supreme.

Her feed is filled with photos of influencers enjoying luxury vacations, driving high-end cars, and working from exotic locations, with captions crediting day trading for their freedom. Jenna becomes captivated by these stories, and each post reinforces her belief that day trading is her ticket out of a financially constrained life.

- The influencers emphasize that anyone can achieve this lifestyle with the "right mindset," saying things like "believe, stay focused, and success will come." Jenna, inspired by their positivity and apparent success, is motivated to start day trading with her own savings, believing she just needs the right attitude and dedication.

2. "Mindset Marketing": The Core of Day Trading's False Positivity

"mindset marketing" has become central to day trading promotions. Influencers and financial "gurus" push the idea that a positive mindset is not only beneficial but essential for trading success.

Key Messages and Tactics in Mindset Marketing: Examples

- o "The only thing holding you back is your mindset."

- o "Success is 90% attitude, 10% action."

- o "If you believe you can do it, nothing will stop you."

Mindset marketing oversimplifies the trading journey, reducing it to an equation of positivity plus determination, while ignoring the critical need for knowledge, strategy, financial stability, and experience. This message is especially misleading because it implies that if traders aren't succeeding, they simply aren't thinking positively enough.

Example: Jenna, after consuming this messaging, decides to begin trading with minimal experience, relying on her confidence and determination to "figure it out as she goes." This leads her to make impulsive trades based on emotional highs rather than strategic planning, setting her up for early losses.

3. The Danger of "Never Give Up" Messaging

Diving into the "never give up" mantra that is widely promoted by influencers, which pushes traders to continue even when faced with mounting losses, implying that perseverance alone will eventually lead to success.

Common Phrases and Themes:

- o "Winners never quit; quitters never win."

- o "Success is just around the corner—don't give up now."

- o "The only way to fail is to stop trying."

This message can be damaging for beginners, who may continue trading out of a sense of obligation to "keep going" even when it's financially harmful. Many traders end up feeling pressured to over-leverage, increase their trade sizes, or even invest more capital, all in an effort to push through.

Case Example:

Jenna begins with a few small losses, which she sees as "tests of her persistence." She tells herself to keep going because that's what successful traders do. She continues to trade, convinced that if she holds on long enough, she'll eventually win back her losses. This belief leads her to pour more money into her account, risking even more despite her growing financial strain.

4. The Isolation and Guilt from Positivity-Driven Culture

The culture of relentless positivity creates a sense of guilt and isolation for traders who experience losses, making them feel as though their struggles are due to personal failings or a lack of positive thinking.

Example:

When Jenna starts facing consistent losses, she feels embarrassed and avoids discussing her challenges with others. She believes her struggles stem from a lack of "right mindset" rather than gaps in her strategy or knowledge. Influencers' messages convince her that she simply needs to "stay positive" to succeed.

This atmosphere discourages traders from sharing honest experiences, as they fear being labeled "negative" or that their struggles will be viewed as personal flaws. This often results in traders feeling isolated, alone in their experiences, and increasingly ashamed of their struggles.

5. The Psychological Impact of "Fake It Till You Make It"

Exploring how the "fake it till you make it" mentality permeates day trading culture, encouraging traders to project an image of success and positivity even if they're struggling or facing losses.

This approach leads many traders to maintain a facade online, often sharing only wins and masking their losses, creating a divide between their online personas and their real experiences.

Example:

Jenna, who has been documenting her trading journey on social media, feels pressured to post only her positive trades and achievements. She shares "inspirational" captions, but internally, she feels like a fraud, struggling to reconcile her online success with her real-life challenges.

This pressure to "fake it" leads to emotional exhaustion and increases anxiety, as traders feel they must live up to their projected image. This stress affects their mental health and leads to poor decision-making as they feel compelled to meet expectations, creating a cycle of stress and underperformance.

6. The Influence of Success Stories and Unrealistic Comparisons

Influencers frequently highlight selective success stories that suggest anyone can achieve immense profits if they maintain a positive outlook and keep going.

No real Influencers name can be used as some brave Whistle Blowers have been sued Millions of Dollars!

Case Study:

An influencer posts about turning a $500 investment into $10,000 in a matter of months, claiming that this success was due to "never giving up" and "believing in the process." However, they fail to mention the risks taken, initial capital invested, or even luck that contributed to this result.

Beginners like Jenna internalize these success stories, believing that they're achievable and feeling inadequate when their results don't match up. They begin to question their commitment or mindset, unaware that these stories represent rare outcomes rather than typical experiences.

These success stories conveniently omit critical factors, such as market conditions, experience level, financial cushion, or even luck, creating an illusion of effortless success that influences new traders to keep chasing similar results.

7. The Pressure to Avoid "Negative" Thinking and Suppress Doubts

Trading communities and forums, often dominated by positive messaging, discourage "negative" discussions, creating an atmosphere where realistic concerns and losses are avoided or dismissed.

<u>Example of Community Pressure:</u>

Jenna, after a string of losses, reaches out to an online community seeking guidance. Instead of helpful feedback, she receives responses like "Stay positive" and "Don't let doubt cloud your vision." This makes her feel as though her concerns are unwelcome or misguided.

This pressure to stay positive isolates traders from discussing real challenges, creating an environment where beginners feel like they must always appear optimistic or risk being shunned by the community.

- Highlighting: this culture not only prevents meaningful learning but also leads to greater financial risks, as traders are discouraged from voicing their doubts, expressing frustration, or acknowledging their losses openly.

8. The Manifestation Myth: When Positivity Leads to Risky Decisions

Analyzing how the concept of "manifestation" is frequently marketed to traders, suggesting that simply visualizing wealth or success can somehow attract financial gains.

While manifestation is rooted in the idea of positive thinking, it becomes misleading when traders are led to believe that mindset alone can drive trading success in a highly volatile, unpredictable market.

Example of the Manifestation Trap:

Jenna begins practicing visualization techniques, convinced that if she imagines herself succeeding, she will attract wealth. She starts taking larger risks, rationalizing that her mindset will "make it work." However, these trades lead to greater losses, and she feels guilt for not "manifesting" hard enough.

- The manifestation myth creates a false sense of control, leading traders to take risks they wouldn't normally consider. When these risks backfire, they often blame themselves for not "believing" hard enough, compounding their financial losses and emotional distress.

9. The Emotional Toll of Constant Positivity

The mental exhaustion that results from trying to maintain an unwaveringly positive outlook in a high-stakes, high-stress environment like day trading.

Example of Emotional Impact:

Jenna, after months of losses and pressure to stay positive, feels burned out and emotionally drained. She struggles with guilt for wanting to quit, fearing that this would make her a "failure." The constant suppression of doubts and worries leaves her feeling hollow and mentally fatigued.

- The relentless positivity promoted by influencers makes traders feel that they must keep going despite financial strain, creating a cycle of stress, doubt, and anxiety. The expectation to remain optimistic even in the face of mounting losses erodes their mental resilience, leading many to feel overwhelmed.

- This mental toll often affects trading performance. Exhausted and disheartened, traders like Jenna become prone to impulsive decisions, risky trades, and emotional reactions, which compound losses and deepen their frustration.

10. The Financial Consequences of "Blind Optimism"

Exploring how the positivity trap can lead to financial consequences, especially for traders who continue to invest money into their accounts, convinced that "staying positive" will eventually lead to success.

Example of Financial Consequences:

Jenna, motivated by the positivity she sees online, continues to add more funds to her account each time she experiences a loss, rationalizing that her belief in herself will turn things around. This cycle of "doubling down" leads to significant financial strain, as she depletes her savings and faces mounting losses.

- Beginners, encouraged by positivity-driven messaging, are often hesitant to stop trading even when it's clear that it's not financially sustainable. Instead, they keep investing, hoping that their optimism and determination will change the outcome.

- This mentality can lead to severe financial repercussions, with beginners exhausting their savings, taking on debt, or even risking essential funds in the belief that positive thinking will eventually yield returns.

Closing: Finding Balance and Embracing Realistic Expectations

Emphasizing that while positivity has value, it cannot replace the importance of strategy, realistic expectations, and risk management in trading.

I encourage readers to seek balanced, honest perspectives and to avoid environments where only wins and positive stories are highlighted. Highlight the importance of finding resources and communities that allow open discussions of both wins and losses.

Chapter 5:

The "Loser Mentality" Myth

1. Opening Story: The Pressure to Succeed in a "Winner's Only" Culture

Example: Begin with Tom, a 30-year-old retail worker who dreams of breaking free from his financial constraints. After discovering day trading through social media, he is inspired by stories of rapid success and the idea that anyone can achieve financial freedom with the right mindset.

Tom joins online communities where people celebrate success but stigmatize failure. Every time he shares a concern, he is told to avoid "thinking like a loser." Members tell him, "You need to commit fully," "No one succeeds with a quitter's mentality," and "Only losers doubt themselves."

Despite putting in long hours to study and trade, Tom finds himself struggling. The pressure to "think like a winner" weighs on him, making each loss feel like a personal failure rather than a part of the learning process.

2. Defining the "Loser Mentality" Myth in Day Trading Culture

The "loser mentality" is characterized in trading culture as any mindset that acknowledges challenges, expresses doubt, or admits mistakes. It's a term used to imply that a trader's struggles are due to personal flaws rather than the high-risk nature of day trading.

The myth fosters a culture of toxic positivity, where failure is stigmatized, and success is glorified as something only those with a "winning mindset" can achieve.

Common Phrases Used to Promote the "Loser Mentality" Myth:

o   "If you're not winning, it's because you're not committed enough."

o   "Winners don't make excuses; losers find reasons to quit."

o   "The only difference between winners and losers is mindset."

- Highlighting that this mentality creates a misleading narrative, suggesting that success in trading is a matter of mindset alone, disregarding the steep learning curve, market unpredictability, and financial risks involved.

3. How Influencers Exploit the "Winner vs. Loser" Mentality

Diving into how influencers leverage the "winner vs. loser" mindset to present themselves as resilient, successful "winners" who overcame adversity, implying that their methods and products can help others do the same.

Influencer Tactics:

Influencers share personal stories of triumph over early failures, claiming they succeeded by shifting to a "winning mentality" and refusing to quit. These narratives imply that those who aren't succeeding just haven't committed to the "winner's mindset."

They sell courses, exclusive memberships, and tools marketed as ways to "transform" a follower's mindset. The implication is that traders can't succeed unless they adopt the influencer's mindset and buy their products.

- This tactic creates dependency. Followers feel that if they don't achieve success, it's because they haven't fully adopted the "winning mindset" taught by the influencer. This fuels an endless cycle of product purchases and membership renewals, benefiting the influencer financially without truly addressing the traders' challenges.

4. The Blame Game: Why Day Trading Losses Are Not Always Personal Failures

Day trading is inherently risky, with frequent losses even for experienced traders. Market fluctuations, timing, and economic factors can significantly impact results, making it unrealistic to expect constant wins.

Example:

Tom diligently prepares for a trade, studying charts and watching the market. However, unexpected economic news causes a market dip, and he loses money. Instead of recognizing that market unpredictability is a natural part of trading, he blames himself, believing he lacks the "winner's mindset" necessary to succeed.

- By promoting the idea that only "losers" fail, trading culture encourages individuals to overlook these real-world challenges and instead internalize failures as personal shortcomings. This leads traders to feel guilty and ashamed, preventing them from making objective adjustments to their strategies.

5. The Psychological Toll of Internalizing the "Loser Mentality" Message

Discussing the emotional toll of constantly hearing that failure is a sign of weakness, lack of commitment, or personal deficiency. Traders start to feel inadequate, isolated, and even depressed when they experience losses.

Example of Emotional Impact:

After several losses, Tom begins feeling anxious and ashamed. He hides his struggles from his friends and family, afraid they'll see him as a "loser." The stress of keeping up a positive facade drains him, and he begins to doubt his self-worth.

- This shame prevents traders from seeking support or discussing losses openly. Instead, they may resort to self-blame, believing they're "not strong enough" or "too weak-minded," which leads to self-isolation and further mental health struggles.

6. The Influence of Exclusive "Winner's Circles" and Mentorship Programs

Many influencers create exclusive groups, mentorships, and "winner's circles" that promise to help members "leave their loser mentality behind." These groups often come with high fees and foster an intense culture of competitiveness.

Example of Group Dynamics:

Members are told that success is only for the dedicated few who are "willing to think like winners." This narrative pressures them to maintain a facade of confidence, regardless of their financial reality. Doubts and concerns are frowned upon, and those who express hesitation are often labeled as having a "loser mindset."

- These groups reinforce the "loser mentality" myth by creating an echo chamber where members feel compelled to hide struggles and continue investing money to maintain their status in the "winner's circle." This setup discourages honest discussions about losses, as members fear being ostracized or seen as "not fully committed."

7. Ignoring Practical Risk Management Due to "Winner's Only" Culture

Discussing how the "winner vs. loser" mentality discourages responsible risk management. Traders are pressured to go "all in" to prove their commitment, often avoiding protective strategies like stop-losses and diversified portfolios.

Example:

Determined to act like a "winner," Tom avoids setting a stop-loss because he's been told that "winners don't hedge their bets." He ends up losing more than he can afford, feeling crushed and defeated. Had he used risk management, his losses could have been minimized.

- By stigmatizing caution and discipline, the "winner's only" culture pushes traders into taking excessive risks, often leading to larger and more damaging losses. Traders feel that stopping or hedging is an admission of doubt or weakness, so they continue trading without adequate safeguards.

8. The Destructive Cycle of Shame, Desperation, and Financial Strain

Exploring how the "loser mentality" myth creates a destructive cycle where traders feel desperate to prove themselves, leading to greater financial strain as they take on more risk to "make up" for past losses.

Example of Desperation:

Tom, embarrassed by his losses and feeling desperate to prove he's not a quitter, begins trading with borrowed funds, hoping to win back his losses. Each additional loss intensifies his feelings of inadequacy, pushing him further into debt and stress.

- Traders get caught in this loop, risking more in an attempt to regain their self-respect. As losses mount, so does the shame, creating a spiral where financial strain and emotional distress feed into each other, making recovery even harder.

9. How the "Loser Mentality" Myth Prevents Honest Reflection and Learning

Successful trading relies on honest reflection and learning from mistakes, but the "loser mentality" myth prevents this by equating self-assessment with weakness.

Example of a Missed Learning Opportunity:

Tom, afraid that analyzing his losses will reveal his "loser mentality," avoids reflecting on his strategies. This prevents him from identifying mistakes, understanding market dynamics, and making adjustments. Instead, he repeats the same errors, prolonging his struggles.

- Highlighting that growth in trading comes from a willingness to assess both successes and failures objectively. By stigmatizing self-reflection, the "loser mentality" myth discourages traders from making necessary improvements and learning from their experiences.

10. Breaking Free: Embracing a Balanced Mindset Over "Loser" Labels

I strongly encourage my readers to reject the "loser mentality" myth and adopt a balanced approach that prioritizes growth, realistic risk management, and continuous learning over rigid ideas of "winning" and "losing."

Healthy Alternatives to the "Loser Mentality" Mindset:

Normalize losses as an inevitable part of trading and see them as opportunities to learn rather than reflections of personal worth.

Embrace risk management practices as essential tools for long-term success. Setting stop-losses, using trade limits, and managing capital responsibly are signs of strength, not weakness.

Seek out communities and mentors who value transparency and allow open discussions about both wins and losses, creating an environment where growth is encouraged over perfection.

- Adopting a balanced mindset leads to healthier trading practices, reduced financial risk, and a stronger sense of self-worth, enabling traders to make strategic decisions without the pressure to constantly "prove" themselves.

11. The Value of Mindful Trading and Self-Compassion

Introducing the concept of mindful trading, where traders approach each trade as an opportunity to learn rather than a high-stakes test of their personal worth.

Practices for Mindful Trading:

View losses as part of the journey, using each as a chance to understand market behavior and adjust strategies.

Recognize the value of taking breaks, recalibrating, and giving oneself permission to step away when necessary. This prevents burnout and encourages a sustainable approach to trading.

Replace self-criticism with self-compassion, understanding that trading is a skill that takes time to develop. Being kind to oneself during setbacks fosters resilience and long-term improvement.

- By practicing self-compassion and mindfulness, traders can engage with the process of trading more openly, allowing themselves to grow without the harsh pressures of a "winner vs. loser" mentality.

12. Reclaiming Control and Learning from the Journey

I encourage my readers to take control of their trading journey by focusing on personal growth, practical learning, and realistic expectations rather than superficial labels of success and failure.

Practical Tips for Reclaiming Control:

Create a journal to track trades, analyzing both wins and losses. This helps identify patterns and allows traders to learn from each experience without judgment.

Set realistic goals and benchmarks, understanding that day trading is a skill that takes time to master. Progress comes from consistency and disciplined learning, not overnight success.

Surround oneself with supportive communities and mentors who provide constructive feedback, encourage honest reflection, and focus on sustainable growth over unrealistic positivity.

- Redefine success on their own terms, recognizing that personal growth, knowledge, and resilience are far more valuable than any "winner" or "loser" label.

Closing: Embracing Growth Over "Winning"

Success in day trading is a continuous journey of learning, self-compassion, and practical growth, not a matter of "winning" or "losing."

Break away from toxic communities that stigmatize failure and instead seek environments that promote balanced, honest approaches to trading.

Chapter 6:

Disposable Income as a Requirement, Not an Option

1. The True Cost of Entry in Day Trading: Beyond the Myths

The Accessibility Illusion:

Many influencers market day trading as a low-barrier activity that anyone with a few hundred dollars can profit from. However, while minimal initial investment may be possible, the reality of sustaining a profitable trading journey is far more expensive. Beginners may not realize that starting with low capital can lead to quick, frequent losses, which require additional funds to recover and continue trading.

The Financial Cushion for Losses:

Unlike long-term investing, day trading requires consistent capital inflows to weather both frequent losses and market fluctuations. Traders who don't have surplus disposable income often find themselves unable to sustain this cycle, which is a key reason why many leave day trading soon after beginning. Without a cushion, traders may also fall into the dangerous habit of "chasing losses," leading to reckless trading decisions.

2. Balancing a Full-Time Job with Day Trading Goals

The Tension Between Time and Volume:

Day trading demands both time and focus. For full-time workers, the lack of available hours during market trading times can prevent effective trade execution, analysis, and learning. This limited availability impacts the number of trades they can execute, reducing their chance of hitting the trade volume needed to produce consistent profits.

Limited Volume Means Limited Returns:

The promise of earning substantial income from day trading often fails to account for the time commitment required to achieve it. Full-time employees often manage only a handful of trades per day, as they balance market monitoring with work commitments. Without enough trades, they cannot maximize profit potential, leading to disappointing returns.

Psychological Toll of Trading in Brief Sessions:

Attempting to day trade in limited time slots adds emotional pressure to every trade, as traders feel compelled to maximize gains within a narrow window. This can lead to impulsive trades or forcing trades in unfavorable conditions, creating a cycle of poor decision-making and potential financial loss.

3. The Realities of Disposable Income and Emotional Pressure

Disposable Income as Essential, Not Optional:

Successful trading relies heavily on disposable income—money that can be risked without impacting essential expenses. For solo-income traders, each dollar spent on trading can increase financial strain if losses occur. Without a steady source of disposable income, losses quickly impact personal budgets, and traders may feel pressure to replenish funds from savings or other essential sources.

Emotional Pressure from Financial Instability:

Traders with insufficient disposable income may find themselves obsessing over every trade outcome. This heightened emotional state often leads to riskier behavior, with traders taking larger or more frequent trades to "make up" for previous losses or low returns. Financial instability exacerbates these issues, creating a pattern of stress that ultimately impairs judgment and decision-making in trading.

4. The Hidden Truth About Day Trading "Experts" and Financial Support

Dual-Income Dependency:

Many self-proclaimed "day trading experts" online rarely mention that they often rely on a secondary income from a spouse or family member. A dual-income setup covers essentials such as rent, utilities, and even incidental trading expenses, giving these "experts" a major advantage. This financial support provides the freedom to trade without risking financial security, which is an advantage not available to many of their followers.

Case Study: A Day Trader with Hidden Support:

Take the example of a YouTube trading expert who promotes their ability to live off day trading income. In reality, their spouse has a full-time job that covers the family's monthly expenses. This second income not only supports basic living costs but allows the trader to dedicate their full income toward trading, absorbing losses without jeopardizing financial stability. This advantage remains hidden from viewers, creating a misleading impression of self-sufficiency.

Selective Transparency and Audience Manipulation:

Many influencers neglect to mention this financial safety net, implying they are financially independent solely from trading. This selective transparency is especially damaging, as beginners may attempt to replicate this supposed "independence" without understanding the role that secondary income support plays in stabilizing their trading ventures.

5. The Mental Strain of Solo-Income Traders: When Every Trade Counts

Amplified Financial Anxiety:

Traders without a secondary income source often experience amplified stress with each trade, as any loss directly affects their personal finances. This anxiety can lead to a "survival mentality," where each decision feels like a high-stakes attempt to protect or grow limited funds. Under such pressure, even minor losses feel monumental, creating a cycle of stress and worry that impacts both mental health and trading judgment.

Isolation and Emotional Fatigue:

Unlike dual-income traders, solo-income traders frequently bear the financial and emotional weight of losses alone. With each setback, they may feel increasingly isolated, discouraged, and reluctant to discuss their struggles with family or friends. This self-isolation leads to emotional fatigue, which only worsens with each unsuccessful trade and ultimately affects their ability to make rational decisions.

The High Price of Overworking:

With minimal disposable income, solo-income traders often feel the need to overtrade to achieve substantial returns. This strategy backfires, as it typically leads to increased financial strain, burnout, and a decline in physical and mental well-being. For full-time workers, this pressure can also lead to distraction or exhaustion in their primary job, causing further stress and potential job insecurity.

6. The Hidden Costs of Time Constraints and Missed Opportunities

Limited Analysis and Increased Error Rates:

Day trading requires diligent analysis of charts, trends, and market behavior. Full-time employees struggle to dedicate sufficient time to properly analyze trades, leading to rushed decisions based on incomplete information. This limited analysis time increases error rates, especially when trying to maximize profit within short sessions.

The Cost of Missing Ideal Trading Hours:

Professional traders typically operate during peak market hours, as these times are known for their highest volatility and trade potential. For part-time or solo-income traders, working hours may prevent access to these critical periods, forcing them to trade during less active times when profit potential is lower. Missing these prime opportunities can further limit earnings and leave traders feeling as if they're "missing out."

The Pressure to Trade in Off-Peak Hours:

Many solo-income traders attempt to trade in after-hours markets to make up for missed opportunities. However, after-hours markets carry heightened risk and volatility, leading to an increased likelihood of losses. Trading during off-peak times can be an additional source of frustration and disappointment, as these markets are often unpredictable and difficult to navigate without extensive experience.

7. Dependency on Spouse's or Family's Support: The Hidden Privilege

Financial Freedom Through Dual-Income Stability:

While some traders can dedicate the entirety of their income to trading, others depend on a spouse or family member's steady income to cover essential expenses. This setup grants freedom and financial stability that solo-income traders cannot easily access. With daily expenses covered, these traders can pursue day trading without fear of compromising their standard of living.

An Overlooked Advantage:

Influencers with hidden support structures frequently imply they are financially independent through trading alone. This creates a false image of success and self-sufficiency that encourages solo-income traders to pursue a level of financial freedom that may be unattainable without a dual-income structure.

Impact of Omitted Financial Privileges on Followers:

Followers often do not know that many influencers benefit from hidden financial security, which changes the stakes of trading significantly. The unmentioned family or spouse income gives influencers a stability cushion that allows them to take more calculated risks without jeopardizing personal finances—an option unavailable to those solely reliant on their own income.

8. The Financial and Emotional Toll of "Going It Alone"

Risk of Overextending Personal Finances:

With limited funds, solo traders may borrow or dip into savings to continue trading after a loss, leading to debt and further financial instability. Without external support, every decision carries higher stakes, intensifying the emotional strain on solo traders, who must be prepared to bear both the financial and emotional costs of failure.

Impact on Personal Relationships and Well-Being:

For solo-income traders, financial pressure often spills into personal relationships, as stress from losses impacts family interactions and increases household tension. Emotional exhaustion and anxiety from day trading can strain relationships, particularly when family members lack understanding of the high-risk environment of day trading.

Psychological Risks of Self-Isolation:

Solo traders often find themselves isolating from friends and family, leading to loneliness and depression. Without a support system, losses feel magnified, and the cycle of isolation worsens. The desire to maintain a positive image to others may push them further into risky decisions as they try to regain confidence and prove themselves successful.

Conclusion: The Overlooked Necessity for Significant Financial and Emotional Backing

Financial Independence in Day Trading Is Rare:

Despite promises of financial freedom, day trading's success rate is low for those without significant financial backing or a second income. For beginners, financial stability and external support are vital.

Transparency Over Hidden Privileges:

By failing to disclose their support systems, influencers mislead their followers. Understanding the importance of disposable income and support can help beginners set realistic expectations and avoid costly, life-altering mistakes.

Final Takeaway:

Financial backing, either through disposable income or dual support, is essential for day trading longevity. Without it, solo traders face heightened risks and an unsustainable cycle of stress, debt, and burnout. Recognizing the true cost of entry can help readers make more informed decisions.

Chapter 7:

The Hidden Costs of 'Learning from the Pros'

1. Introduction: The Lure of Expert Knowledge and the Promise of a Shortcut

The allure of expert guidance is a powerful motivator, particularly for beginners who find the world of day trading complex and intimidating. Day trading "pros" often market themselves as guides who can simplify this journey, promising that their insights will help newcomers bypass the difficult learning curve. With slick advertising, they create an illusion of accessibility, portraying day trading as a skill anyone can master if they have access to the right knowledge and guidance.

The real danger lies in the tendency of followers to grow loyal to a single "professional." Many beginners begin with the belief that listening to just one guru will eliminate confusion and increase their chances of success. This belief leads them to invest in every course, book, and product the expert releases, and even buy their branded merchandise as a symbol of devotion and commitment. Over time, they begin to disregard alternative perspectives, funneling their trust and money into one individual's vision.

This exclusivity not only stunts their growth but also traps them in a cycle of spending. They begin to believe that they're just one course, tool, or product away from reaching their breakthrough moment. This unending loop of dependency is profitable for the "pro," who profits from the follower's desire for shortcuts—but for the beginner, it often leads to disappointment and financial strain.

2. The Cost of Courses and Educational Programs

Courses are often the first step in a beginner's journey into the world of day trading, and financial gurus take full advantage of this by presenting their courses as life-changing educational experiences. Advertisements for these courses usually claim that beginners can "fast-track" their success, implying that a few hundred dollars' worth of lessons will give them the insights needed to achieve financial freedom.

While the initial courses may seem affordable, they're frequently just an entry point into a much larger, more expensive ecosystem. Basic courses are usually packed with general information and foundational knowledge, but they deliberately leave out detailed strategies. Instead, the beginner is led to believe that true "insider secrets" are only available at the next level, usually a more expensive intermediate or advanced course.

Case Study:

Imagine Jane, a 29-year-old who has been drawn to day trading as a side income. She begins with a $250 introductory course that promises to teach her "everything she needs to know." However, upon completion, she feels that the material barely scratches the surface. The expert then markets an intermediate course for $750, claiming it holds the key to advanced strategies. Jane, wanting to make her initial investment worthwhile, decides to take this course, only to find that it's yet another stepping stone to an "exclusive" $2,000 advanced course. By the time Jane realizes the pattern, she has spent over $1,000 and still lacks practical skills. Her financial resources are drained, and her confidence is shaken.

This structure is by design, intended to create a continuous upsell cycle. Each course promotes the next level, framing it as a critical step for those "serious" about day trading. In reality, the information shared is often the same general knowledge available for free online, rephrased to create a sense of exclusivity.

3. Mentorship and Coaching Programs

For beginners with a larger budget, financial gurus offer exclusive mentorship and coaching programs, often marketed as the ultimate resource for mastering day trading. Unlike courses, which are typically pre-recorded and self-paced, mentorship programs promise one-on-one support, implying that direct access to the expert's advice will finally unlock success. The personalization is enticing, as beginners believe that tailored guidance will address their unique challenges and speed up their progress.

However, these mentorships are notoriously expensive, with prices ranging from $5,000 to well over $10,000. They're framed as high-value experiences, where participants become part of an elite group, creating a sense of exclusivity and social status. Mentorships offer a psychological reward in addition to the promise of financial gain: being "chosen" for one of these programs makes followers feel valued, reinforcing loyalty to the expert and solidifying a sense of dependency.

Yet, the reality of these mentorships often doesn't live up to the hype. Mentorship programs typically recycle the same advice available in the courses, focusing on vague concepts like "positive mindset," "staying the course," and "reading the market."

Beginners rarely gain actionable insights that translate into real-world trading success. Instead, they're left with general tips that could apply to anyone, diminishing the value of the mentorship.

Reinforced Devotion and Exclusivity:

By creating a sense of belonging, the expert encourages participants to stick with their guidance, even when results are lacking. If a beginner has invested $10,000 in personal coaching, they're far less likely to walk away or explore alternative perspectives—they're too financially and emotionally invested to admit the guidance may be insufficient. As a result, they continue to purchase new products, trusting that the expert knows what's best, even as their progress stagnates.

4. The Never-Ending Subscription Fees for Tools and Data

Beyond courses and mentorship, many "pros" promote specialized tools and real-time data feeds as essential components of a successful trading strategy. These tools include charting software, real-time market data, and even algorithmic trading programs. Each of these products is presented as indispensable for anyone who wants to "trade like a pro," and beginners are often told that without these tools, they're at a serious disadvantage.

These tools, however, come with significant recurring fees. Subscriptions can range from $50 to $200 a month or more, quickly adding up to thousands of dollars each year. For beginners who haven't yet generated consistent profits, these monthly costs can be overwhelming and financially draining, especially when combined with the costs of courses and mentorships.

Example of Monthly Costs:

Let's say a beginner signs up for a charting tool at $100 per month, a premium data feed at $120, and a risk management tool at $60. That's a total of $280 per month, or $3,360 annually. For someone with a small trading account, these costs can consume any profits they make, leaving them no closer to financial freedom.

The real irony is that many beginners don't need these advanced tools when they're just starting out. Free or low-cost alternatives can often meet their needs while they learn the basics. However, by promoting these tools as essential, the expert creates a perception that anyone serious about day trading must be willing to invest heavily in technology.

5. Affiliate Marketing and Biased Recommendations

Unbeknownst to many beginners, financial "pros" are frequently incentivized to promote specific tools and platforms through affiliate marketing. This means they earn commissions each time a follower subscribes to a recommended tool, often without the follower knowing that the recommendation is financially motivated. While this in itself isn't necessarily unethical, it becomes problematic when the expert prioritizes personal profit over the beginner's best interests.

Instead of providing unbiased advice, these experts endorse tools that may be costly or overly complex for beginners. The follower, unaware of this financial arrangement, assumes that the recommendation is based solely on merit. This affiliate-based structure perpetuates a cycle of spending, where the beginner believes they must keep purchasing the expert's recommended products to increase their chances of success.

Example of Affiliate Marketing:

Consider an expert who promotes a $200-per-month charting tool, calling it "indispensable" for day trading. This tool may be more advanced than the beginner needs, but the expert fails to mention alternative, lower-cost options. The beginner subscribes, and the expert earns a commission, creating an incentive to push products that generate profit—even if they aren't truly beneficial for beginners.

6. The Psychological Pressure to Invest in 'Essential' Knowledge

The marketing behind these courses, tools, and mentorships is designed to create a psychological urgency that plays on the fear of missing out (FOMO). Many gurus frame their programs as limited-time offers or exclusive opportunities, suggesting that without these resources, beginners will be left behind in a fast-paced market. This creates an intense pressure to keep investing, leading beginners to spend more money out of a sense of obligation and fear.

For beginners struggling to see progress, this pressure is compounded by guilt and self-blame. They may start to believe that they're failing because they haven't invested enough in themselves, creating a cycle of financial and emotional strain. As they continue to pour money into programs and tools, the financial burden increases, but the actual impact on their trading success remains limited.

7. The Minimal Impact on Trading Success

After spending thousands of dollars on courses, tools, and mentorship programs, many beginners come to a disheartening realization: the impact on their trading success is minimal. Despite the promises of "transformative knowledge," most of what these experts offer is general information that fails to address the unique challenges of day trading in real-time.

Example of False Advertising:

Many beginners report feeling just as lost as when they started, despite having completed multiple courses and mentorship programs. The advertised "secrets" turn out to be vague principles like "buy low, sell high" or broad advice on market psychology. For the beginner, this is a letdown, as they expected specific strategies and techniques that could lead to actual profits.

This disappointment isn't just financial—it's emotional. The beginner, who has spent significant time and money in pursuit of success, begins to feel betrayed, as they realize the "insider knowledge" they purchased was little more than surface-level advice dressed up as proprietary information.

8. Affordable Alternatives: Learning Basics Through Low-Cost Books and Free Online Content

For those who take a step back, there are alternative paths to learning day trading that don't require heavy financial investment. Much of the foundational knowledge is available through inexpensive or even free resources, allowing beginners to educate themselves without the added stress of expensive purchases.

Inexpensive E-Books and Guides:

Many beginner-friendly e-books on platforms like Amazon cover essential day trading topics, from technical analysis to psychology, for as little as $10. These e-books provide a solid foundation and often offer the same insights as pricier courses.

Free Resources on YouTube and Websites:

YouTube hosts countless free tutorials and trading explanations, with reputable channels dedicated to educating beginners. Additionally, websites like Investopedia offer in-depth articles and tutorials on trading fundamentals, all at no cost.

Encouraging beginners to explore these options can prevent them from feeling pressured to invest in every paid product they encounter. Free and low-cost resources can give beginners a realistic understanding of day trading without the financial burden, helping them approach the field with a balanced perspective.

Conclusion: Recognizing Genuine Value vs. Sales Tactics

Success in day trading can't be bought through a shortcut. While expert guidance can be valuable, beginners should approach each product and service with caution, carefully evaluating whether it offers unique value. Much of the knowledge needed for day trading is available for free or through affordable resources, making it unnecessary to rely solely on the promises of paid "pros."

Real progress in day trading requires consistent practice, self-discipline, and a willingness to learn independently. Beginners who adopt a cautious approach and seek a well-rounded education are more likely to succeed than those who chase paid "secrets." Ultimately, the journey to becoming a successful trader is about patience, perseverance, and developing one's skills—not paying for shortcuts that rarely deliver as promised.

Chapter 8:

The Scaling Up Trap: The Emotional Toll of Day Trading

1. The Temptation and Danger of Scaling Up

The False Sense of Control:

When new traders experience early wins, it often reinforces a false sense of mastery over the market. This illusion encourages them to risk larger sums, believing they can repeat their successes.

Shifts from Small to Large Stakes:

For many, the journey begins with a series of small trades, but as they become frustrated with minimal returns, they start to take larger positions. These decisions often come with intense pressure, knowing that one significant loss could wipe out any small gains they've made.

The Cycle of Escalating Risks:

As traders scale up, they often feel a sense of urgency to "make it back" on the next trade. The pressure to recoup losses through larger trades becomes a recurring trap, as the stakes continue to grow higher and the emotional toll intensifies.

2. The Mental Exhaustion of Constantly Calculating Costs

The Hidden Math of Trading Costs:

Expanding on platform fees, commissions, and hidden charges, we could include examples of how these costs compound over time. Imagine a trader who makes dozens of trades per week, each one with fees that eat into potential profits. The constant realization that every trade has to "make up" for these fees drains enthusiasm and hope.

Calculating Break-Even Points:

To fully appreciate how much they need to just break even, traders often find themselves doing complex mental math on every trade. This constant arithmetic wears down even the most motivated individuals, creating a mental load that overshadows any small wins they achieve.

3. The Emotional Roller Coaster of Wins and Losses

The Short-Lived Highs of Winning Trades:

In day trading, wins can be exhilarating—but they're fleeting. Expanding on the emotional highs, describe how a successful trade gives a rush that dissipates almost immediately as traders search for the next opportunity. Instead of celebrating, they're pulled back into the search for new trades to sustain their "winning streak."

Catastrophic Losses:

Losses feel exponentially more painful as stakes increase. Adding an example of a large loss, such as someone losing a significant part of their trading account in a single day, highlights the despair and self-doubt that follow. Traders who lose big often experience an emotional spiral, replaying the decisions they made and obsessing over what they could have done differently.

The Psychological Toll of a Losing Streak:

When losses happen in succession, traders often feel trapped, unable to reverse their fortunes. The feeling of being on a losing streak amplifies doubt, making it hard to see any way out.

4. Anxiety and Physical Health Decline

The Perpetual Worry Loop:

Anxiety doesn't just exist during trading hours. Traders carry their stress home with them, feeling uneasy and tense as they try to anticipate what the next day will bring. This emotional load often manifests as physical symptoms like chronic headaches, stomach issues, and tension in the body.

Addiction to Market Monitoring:

Even when markets close, traders obsess over news, trends, and possible overnight changes. This habit disturbs sleep, with some traders waking in the middle of the night to check international markets. The lack of restful sleep begins to wear down their mental resilience, making them more prone to irrational decisions.

Health Impacts of Screen Time:

Day traders often spend hours in front of screens, resulting in issues like eye strain, headaches, and poor posture. These physical issues combine with mental stress, creating a feedback loop that slowly deteriorates their overall health.

5. Relationship Strains: The Hidden Impact of Financial Stress

Isolation from Loved Ones:

As traders spend more time glued to their screens, family and friends feel pushed aside. Relationships suffer when traders become withdrawn, emotionally unavailable, and preoccupied with their financial struggles. Loved ones may notice that the trader is "present in body but absent in mind."

The Unspoken Shame of Losses:

Many traders feel embarrassed discussing their financial losses with family, especially if they initially portrayed day trading as a path to success. As losses mount, they avoid conversations about money or plans for the future, leaving loved ones concerned and feeling disconnected.

Erosion of Trust:

Family members may lose trust in the trader, particularly when financial strain affects shared expenses. The secrecy around losses or debts taken on to fund trading can create rifts in relationships, leading to resentment and feelings of betrayal.

6. The Trap of "Expert" Advice That Backfires

The Emotional Whiplash of Following Bad Tips:

For many beginners, advice from so-called experts is a safety net. When this advice fails, they experience emotional whiplash, feeling betrayed by the very people they trusted. Each bad trade resulting from poor guidance becomes a reminder of the money and time they've lost.

Constant Search for the "Right" Mentor:

The back-and-forth of following conflicting expert opinions creates a sense of confusion and helplessness. Traders feel as though they're perpetually in search of someone who can "unlock" the secrets to success, a cycle that saps their confidence and leaves them questioning their own instincts.

7. Trading Addiction and the Cycle of Compulsive Behavior

The Lure of a "Big Win":

Many traders who feel trapped in losses see a big win as their salvation. This leads to increasingly risky decisions as they attempt to "hit it big" and get out of the hole. The thrill of risk-taking becomes addictive, and they chase this feeling, often to their own detriment.

Denial of Losses:

Much like gambling addicts, some traders refuse to accept their losses. Instead of acknowledging the harm trading is causing, they convince themselves they're "one trade away" from a breakthrough. This denial deepens their losses, pushing them further into debt or depletion of their resources.

Signs of Addiction:

Common signs include feeling an overwhelming need to trade, inability to focus on other tasks, and feeling irritable or restless when away from the market. As this addiction progresses, it consumes their life, leaving them emotionally drained and financially compromised.

8. Case Studies of Traders in the Scaling Up Trap

Personal Story of a Trader's Downfall:

Including a story about a real-life trader who escalated their trades and lost a significant portion of their savings could add emotional depth. For example, a story about a trader who started with a few small wins but spiraled into debt as they attempted to replicate those wins at a higher scale. This case study can highlight the gradual transition from cautious trading to all-consuming risk-taking.

Psychological Impact of Failure:

Describing a trader's journey from initial optimism to desperation and regret paints a vivid picture of the psychological costs involved. Detail the moment they realize their financial and emotional investments haven't paid off, capturing the feelings of disappointment, guilt, and loss.

Conclusion: The Price of Scaling Up

The Long Road to Recovery:

Many traders who experience the scaling up trap need a prolonged period to recover financially and emotionally. This recovery is often painful, involving the rebuilding of savings, relationships, and self-confidence. The process requires them to confront the emotional scars left by their experience in the market.

Acknowledging the Bitter Reality:

I urge my readers to see the reality behind the glamorized version of day trading. Emphasizing the genuine mental and physical sacrifices involved will serve as a sobering reminder that day trading isn't a shortcut to wealth but a high-stakes endeavor that many don't emerge from unscathed.

Chapter 9:

The Unique Costs of Professional Day Trading Equipment

1. Introduction: The Often-Ignored Financial Burden of Day Trading Tools

Setting Up the Expectation vs. Reality Dilemma

Many aspiring traders are lured into day trading by promises of low-cost entry and significant profits. The upfront investment might seem manageable, perhaps only a few hundred dollars to set up an account. However, the reality of staying competitive in the high-speed, technology-driven world of day trading reveals an ongoing, significant financial burden that quickly catches beginners off guard.

The Reality Check

Most beginners enter day trading without understanding the true cost of required tools and technology. While they might budget their initial trading capital, they fail to account for expenses such as high-performance hardware, specialized software, recurring data fees, and ergonomic workspaces. This chapter opens with the story of *Alex*, a newcomer who thought he was financially prepared with a $1,000 account, only to be overwhelmed by the mounting costs of the necessary tools to maintain a professional trading setup.

2. High-Performance Computers and Software: The Core of Professional Trading

Why Day Traders Can't Rely on Regular Laptops

Day trading demands processing speed, stability, and capacity for multiple applications running simultaneously. Unlike standard work or personal computers, day trading machines must handle real-time data and execute orders within milliseconds to capitalize on rapid market shifts. A standard laptop is prone to lag or even crash under these demands, leading to missed opportunities or, worse, financial losses.

Cost Breakdown for High-End Equipment

Professional setups often require a robust CPU (costing between $300 and $1,500), ample RAM (at least 16GB, costing $100+), and a high-performance GPU ($500-$1,500). Additionally, solid-state drives (SSDs) are essential for quick data retrieval and can add another $100-$500.

Example Story: Laura's Investment

Laura, a beginner trader, initially spent $2,500 on a desktop setup, thinking it would last for years. Within two years, however, she found herself needing to upgrade her GPU and add more RAM to keep up with software demands, costing her an additional $800. For traders like Laura, the realization that hardware requires ongoing upgrades comes as a frustrating—and costly—surprise.

3. Multi-Monitor Setups: An Essential for the Serious Trader

Why Multiple Screens are Necessary

A multi-monitor setup allows traders to view different assets, charts, and market news simultaneously, enabling quick, informed decisions. For serious traders, switching between tabs on a single screen is inefficient and increases the risk of missing critical market moves.(for advanced traders, not beginners!)

Setting Up a Multi-Monitor Workstation
A professional-grade setup may include 3-6 monitors, each costing $150-$500, with additional ergonomic monitor stands at $100-$300. Mounts or stands to arrange these monitors comfortably can add another layer of expense, especially when space is limited.

Example of Multi-Monitor Costs
Consider a setup with four monitors at $300 each, a sturdy stand at $200, and a specialized desk costing $500. The initial cost of $1,900 for a multi-monitor setup is a significant investment, and ergonomic replacements or upgrades add to the ongoing expense.

Health Costs for Ergonomics
Due to the extended hours, ergonomic workspaces become crucial. Long hours in front of multiple screens can strain the body, leading to neck, back, or eye problems. Investing in a good ergonomic chair ($300-$1,200) and desk, which might cost another $500 or more, becomes necessary for health and productivity, adding to the financial burden.

4. Subscription Fees for Real-Time Market Data: The Hidden Monthly Cost

Why Real-Time Data is Non-Negotiable
In day trading, data that is even slightly delayed can lead to financial losses. Real-time data feeds provide up-to-the-second information on stock prices, trends, and market volume, which is essential for making split-second decisions.

Breakdown of Subscription Options

Platforms like Bloomberg Terminal offer high-end solutions at around $2,000/month. For traders seeking more affordable options, platforms like TradingView or Eikon charge $50-$500/month depending on the level of data and analysis tools. These monthly expenses quickly accumulate, especially for traders who initially expected only a single upfront cost.

Real Story of Costs

Sam, a new trader, started with a basic $100/month subscription, which seemed reasonable. However, as he expanded his trading strategies, he needed premium data feeds and additional tools, increasing his monthly expense to $300. After a year, this $3,600 cost surprised him, as he hadn't anticipated such an ongoing financial burden.

5. Specialized Risk Management and Trading Analysis Tools

The Need for Advanced Risk Management

Professional day traders often use automated risk management tools to set limits on their trades and minimize losses. Additionally, software for backtesting, real-time analysis, and automated trading strategies help traders make informed decisions.

Cost of Subscription-Based Tools

These tools are rarely free, and professional versions can range from $50 to $500 monthly. Beginners often start with basic tools, but the perceived need to "upgrade" grows as they become more familiar with day trading. This gradual increase in monthly expenses leads to unexpected financial strain.

Case Study: The Cost of Progress

Alex, after spending $1,200 on a year of software subscriptions, decided to upgrade to professional-level tools, adding another $2,000 to his expenses. This scenario reflects how traders are constantly incentivized to purchase additional tools, believing they will make a difference in their profits—often to no avail.

Constant Need for Upgrades to Stay Competitive

The Pressure to Keep Technology Updated

Trading technology evolves rapidly, with new software and hardware coming out frequently. Even with an initial investment, traders find themselves upgrading every few years to avoid lag or inefficiencies.

Financial Impact of Upgrades

Traders can expect to spend $500-$1,000 every 1-2 years on hardware upgrades alone, in addition to software subscription updates. This cumulative cost adds up over time, representing a hidden expense that may negate a substantial portion of annual profits.

Real-Life Example of Ongoing Upgrades

Chris, who began with a $3,000 setup, has spent an additional $2,500 on upgrades over five years. For him, the financial impact is substantial, as these costs eat into his profits, making it difficult to justify the initial low-cost appeal of day trading.

7. Home Office Requirements for Stability and Focus

Necessity of a Dedicated Trading Space

Day trading from home requires a distraction-free environment with secure, reliable internet. Traders may invest in soundproofing, a high-quality ergonomic setup, and fast internet, especially if they rely solely on day trading for income.

High-Speed Internet and Backup Systems

High-speed internet at $100-$200/month is essential, often supplemented by a mobile hotspot backup for $50/month to prevent financial losses from connection failures.

Real Story of Internet Costs

Evan experienced an internet outage during a critical trade, resulting in a loss. Afterward, he invested in a dual-connection system, spending $200/month on a primary and backup internet, realizing the added cost was essential for avoiding future losses.

8. Hidden Impact of Equipment and Software on Profit Margins

Monthly Financial Overview

A typical day trader's monthly expenses could include $300 for data feeds, $200 for software, $150 for backup internet, and $50 for hardware upgrades—a total of $700/month. Annualized, this $8,400 in overheads can wipe out a significant percentage of profits.

The Reality of High Overhead Costs

New traders like *Jane*, who entered with limited capital, find that these overheads mean profits are often minimal after expenses. Even with consistent wins, the high recurring costs prevent real growth, creating a financial treadmill that drains rather than builds wealth.

9. Affordable Alternatives and When to Upgrade

Risk of Using Outdated or Free Tools

While free tools exist, they may be unreliable or lack the speed and data accuracy needed for serious trading. Delayed or limited data can hurt trade timing, causing beginners to miss opportunities.

Practical Advice for Cost-Effective Solutions

Beginners might start with basic tools like free charting platforms and upgrade only when consistent profits justify it. Traders are advised to avoid the "tech trap" until necessary, using affordable tools while they hone their skills and transition gradually.

When to Invest Heavily

Advising that traders only upgrade when the potential profits justify the expense. For instance, transitioning to higher-end data feeds or professional software only once monthly profits consistently surpass these additional costs.

Conclusion: Recognizing the Financial Realities of Day Trading Overhead

Transparency in Day Trading Expenses

I Encourage traders to take these recurring costs seriously when budgeting. Success in day trading is not just about skill but about managing overhead costs, which can consume a significant percentage of potential profits.

Setting Up for the Next Chapter

Concluding, these expenses are frequently overlooked by online gurus, who portray day trading as a "low investment" opportunity. This chapter paves the way for the following chapter's discussion on how influencers and experts manipulate these misconceptions to lure new traders into the market.

Chapter 10:

Financial Gurus and the Illusion of Guaranteed Success

1. Introduction: The Allure of Financial Gurus

The Social Media "Experts" Phenomenon

In the age of social media, financial "gurus" have become some of the most compelling figures online. With carefully constructed personal brands, these influencers capitalize on the universal desire for financial independence, promising to reveal the "secrets" of wealth. They position themselves as relatable success stories—people who were once struggling, just like their followers, but who found an "easy way out." They tell stories of their own supposed success through day trading or other high-yield investments, creating a false sense of hope and inspiration.

How They Captivate Audiences

These gurus use high-impact storytelling, building a narrative arc that seems both relatable and aspirational. They might share details of how they were once in deep debt, struggling with dead-end jobs, or barely making ends meet. This vulnerability draws followers in, making the guru appear genuine. However, it's this very relatability that ultimately becomes a hook, leading followers to believe, "If they can do it, so can I." Through personal anecdotes, lifestyle posts, and testimonials, they foster a deep emotional connection, making their followers more susceptible to their pitches.

2. Selling the Illusion of 'Insider' Knowledge

The Psychological Appeal of 'Exclusive' Access

Financial gurus know that people are drawn to the idea of "secret" or "exclusive" knowledge. By claiming to offer "insider" tips that are unavailable to the average person, they create an allure that makes followers feel like they're accessing forbidden knowledge. Terms like "only a few people know this" or "I can't share this with just anyone" are used to suggest exclusivity and privilege, tapping into a desire for special access and power.

The Hidden Costs of These "Secrets"

While these gurus may initially charge a small fee for access, this is often just the tip of the iceberg. They strategically introduce more advanced courses, special coaching sessions, and premium content that costs hundreds or even thousands of dollars, all under the promise of "unlocking the next level." However, as followers progress through these courses, they often find little new or groundbreaking information. Instead, they encounter rehashed content and motivational platitudes designed to keep them coming back for more, leading to an endless cycle of spending without tangible returns.

- **Example: The "Endless Ladder" Strategy**
  Sophia, a young professional, spent $300 on a beginner's day trading course advertised by a popular guru. Convinced by

the marketing, she believed this course was the first step toward unlocking financial freedom. However, the course was full of vague concepts and general information, leading her to feel like she needed the "next level" course, priced at $1,000. By the time Sophia realized she wasn't gaining any real, actionable knowledge, she had spent over $5,000, feeling frustrated and financially strained.

3. Investment Schemes: Handing Over Money to the Guru

The Temptation of 'Managed' Investments

Some gurus go a step further, persuading followers to hand over their money to be "managed" directly by them. These gurus promise that they'll invest the money on their followers' behalf, using their supposedly superior knowledge to yield substantial returns. Followers are led to believe that these gurus' lower fees will save them money compared to traditional financial advisors, making it seem like a smart, cost-effective choice.

The Dangers of Handing Over Control

These managed investments often come with vague explanations, lacking transparency about where and how the money is invested. In the worst cases, followers discover that their funds were never invested at all and that the guru used them for personal gain or risky, high-stakes bets that left them with nothing. This experience not only leads to financial devastation but also leaves followers with feelings of betrayal, guilt, and shame for having trusted someone who presented themselves as a financial savior.

- **Case Example: Betrayal and Loss**
  James, a single parent looking to secure a future for his

children, sent $15,000 to a guru who promised to double his money within a year. Assured by the guru's daily posts of luxury and success, James trusted this "expert" to make sound investments. But after several months of silence, James discovered that his account was empty. The guru, claiming market downturns, blamed "unforeseen" events but took no responsibility. This betrayal left James feeling deeply deceived and financially devastated.

4. The Illusion of Wealth: Staged Success and Fabricated Testimonials

Curated Displays of Wealth and Success

Financial gurus create an illusion of wealth by showcasing luxurious lifestyles—fast cars, high-end hotels, designer clothes—that their followers are told are the rewards of successful day trading. But what they don't reveal is that these luxuries are often rented or borrowed solely for the purpose of marketing. Followers assume that the lavish lifestyle is proof of trading success, making it easier for them to rationalize the high cost of courses or direct investments.

False Testimonials from 'Successful' Students

To reinforce the guru's success narrative, many testimonials are fabricated or sourced from actors paid to create glowing reviews. These testimonials are crafted to sound relatable, convincing followers that others like them have achieved success by following the guru's advice. When followers see people they perceive as ordinary and similar to themselves supposedly finding success, they're more likely to buy into the narrative and feel that their own dreams of financial freedom are achievable.

- **Example of Manipulation: Katie's Journey**

  Katie, a recent college graduate, saw a series of testimonials from young adults who claimed they made thousands within months after joining a guru's trading program. Intrigued and inspired, Katie spent $1,500 on a course. Later, she found out from online forums that the "students" in these testimonials were paid actors. Feeling humiliated and exploited, Katie realized the extent of the manipulation that led her into the program.

5. Affiliate Marketing and Biased Recommendations

Affiliate Marketing Behind the Scenes

Many financial gurus promote specific trading tools, platforms, and software, describing them as essential for trading success. However, what they don't disclose is that they receive a commission for every follower who subscribes to these services. This biased recommendation often leads followers to invest in costly tools they may not need, further enriching the guru while adding another expense to the follower's budget.

Realizing the Cost of Biased Advice

A follower may be directed to subscribe to premium trading software, costing hundreds per month, or to invest in high-fee platforms. These costs add up quickly and can consume any profits the follower might earn, leaving them financially worse off. Many only realize the profit-driven nature of these recommendations after they've already invested heavily in tools that don't suit their needs.

- **Example of Financial Drain: Alex's Experience**

  Alex, a part-time retail worker, was convinced by his favorite trading guru that a specific $200/month trading tool was "essential" for success. After months of costly subscriptions, Alex realized that similar free tools existed. When he discovered the guru's affiliate relationship with the software, Alex felt used, frustrated at the money he'd lost to biased advice.

6. Emotional Manipulation: Targeting Hope, Fear, and Desperation

Using Emotion to Drive Urgency

Financial gurus are adept at reading people's emotions, particularly those who are financially vulnerable. They craft messages that create a sense of urgency, using phrases like "don't miss out on this opportunity" or "time is running out." This urgency taps into followers' fear of missing a chance at financial security, manipulating them into making impulsive decisions.

Preying on the Desire for a Better Future

These gurus often speak directly to people's deepest hopes and insecurities, promising a way out of dead-end jobs, debt, or financial stress. They paint an idealized picture of life post-success, suggesting that followers are only one investment, course, or strategy away from changing their lives. For those already feeling hopeless or trapped, this dream is a powerful lure.

- **Example: Sarah's Investment out of Desperation**
  Sarah, a single mother barely making ends meet, invested in a high-priced mentorship program after seeing the guru's message, "Don't wait until it's too late." She used credit to cover the cost, believing the promise of quick returns. When the mentorship failed to deliver, Sarah was left in debt and filled with regret, realizing she'd been manipulated at a vulnerable time.

7. Stories of Financial and Emotional Ruin

The Financial and Emotional Toll

Many who follow financial gurus experience not only financial loss but also emotional devastation. The shame, guilt, and anger from being deceived are compounded by the loss of hard-earned money. Some followers even experience mental health struggles as they grapple with feelings of betrayal and self-doubt, questioning how they allowed themselves to be misled.

- **Example: Mark's Journey from Hope to Disillusionment**
  Mark, a mid-career professional, drained his savings to follow a guru's trading strategies, thinking it would provide a better future for his family. When the promises fell apart, he struggled with severe depression, feeling as though he'd failed not only himself but his loved ones as well. The emotional toll of realizing he'd been exploited was as devastating as the financial loss.

8. Recognizing Red Flags and Safeguarding Against Deceptive Practices

Warning Signs to Watch Out For

Emphasizing common red flags: promises of high returns with low risk, emphasis on secrecy and exclusivity, high-pressure sales tactics, testimonials without verifiable sources, and heavy promotion of specific tools or services. Readers are encouraged to approach these signs with caution and skepticism.

Strategies for Verification and Protection

Ways you can protect yourself, such as researching a guru's background, checking for independent reviews, asking about qualifications, and seeking advice from multiple sources before committing money. By taking these steps, can you ensure they are making informed, rational decisions.

Conclusion: Taking Back Control and Building Financial Resilience

Reclaiming Trust in Personal Judgment

True financial success isn't about shortcuts but about steady, informed decisions and personal growth. By avoiding the allure of quick fixes and focusing on long-term strategies, readers can build their financial futures without falling victim to exploitative practices.

Empowering Financial Independence

Seek reputable, affordable resources, prioritize financial literacy, and trust in their own ability to make sound financial decisions. With time, effort, and discipline, they can pursue financial growth without reliance on deceptive gurus.

Chapter 11:

The Hidden Costs of Professional Day Trading Equipment

1. Introduction: The High-Stakes Setup of Professional Day Trading

Beyond the "Laptop Lifestyle" Fantasy

Influencers and financial "gurus" frequently portray day trading as a flexible, low-maintenance career that anyone can pursue from a coffee shop or a simple home office. Photos of minimalist setups and inspirational captions feed the myth of a glamorous, accessible path to financial independence. But the reality of professional day trading involves a costly setup that goes far beyond a single laptop on a sleek desk.

The Financial Reality of Setting Up for Success

Serious day traders know that success requires a complex, high-performing setup that can handle the demands of fast-paced markets. Multiple screens, high-speed internet, specialized ergonomic furniture, and ongoing software subscriptions all add up quickly, creating a hefty overhead. For beginners, the revelation of these hidden costs is often shocking, and many find themselves overwhelmed by the financial and emotional burden these investments create. Without a well-funded trading account, this setup can quickly become a source of stress rather than a path to profits.

2. High-Performance Computers and Software: The Heart of Trading

The Requirement for High-Speed Processing Power

In day trading, processing speed is critical. Basic computers and laptops don't have the processing power to run complex trading software, charts, and real-time data analysis smoothly. Traders need advanced, high-speed computers with ample RAM, solid-state drives (SSDs), and multi-core processors to handle large datasets and maintain system stability. This kind of high-performance hardware is essential, as even a brief system freeze or lag can lead to missed opportunities and costly errors.

The Substantial Investment in Computer Hardware

A high-performance setup isn't cheap. A reliable day trading computer with sufficient specs can cost $1,500 to $3,000 or more. Even with this investment, traders frequently need upgrades to maintain their system's effectiveness, with processors, graphics cards, and storage regularly needing enhancement as software becomes more demanding. The constant need for updates often turns an initial one-time expense into an ongoing investment.

- **Example: Ben's Battle with Lag and Lost Trades**

  Ben, a new trader, started with a budget-friendly computer, thinking it would be sufficient for his day trading needs. However, his system began lagging during high-volume market times, causing delays in executing trades. Frustrated, he upgraded to a $2,500 high-speed desktop, only to realize he needed further upgrades to his storage and processing speed to handle multiple trading platforms. The total cost left him financially strained, and the constant need to stay technologically up-to-date weighed on him, transforming trading from an opportunity into a costly race to keep up with his setup.

3. Multiple Monitors: The Essential Eyes of a Trader

Why Multiple Monitors Are Necessary

Unlike conventional office work, day trading requires traders to monitor various charts, indicators, and live news feeds simultaneously. Professional traders often use multiple screens to track assets, trends, and news in real time, creating an efficient workspace that helps them make quick decisions. A single screen limits visibility, making it nearly impossible to keep up with market data as it changes by the second.

Financial Commitment for a Multi-Monitor Setup

High-quality monitors cost between $200 and $400 each, and most professional setups use at least three to four monitors. Traders also need monitor stands or specialized desks to support the weight and setup of multiple screens, bringing the total cost for a multi-monitor setup to $1,500 or more.

- **Example: Sophie's Escalating Monitor Costs**
  Sophie began day trading with a basic dual-monitor setup, but she quickly found herself overwhelmed by the constant window-switching needed to follow charts, news feeds, and market data. She added two more screens to her setup, investing an additional $800 in monitors and a desk designed

for multi-monitor setups. However, each screen served as a constant reminder of her financial investment, amplifying her anxiety whenever she took a loss. Over time, the strain of needing each trade to justify her setup costs wore on her, turning her monitors into symbols of her financial risk.

4. Reliable, High-Speed Internet: The Necessity No One Talks About

Why High-Speed Internet is Non-Negotiable

Day traders rely on speed and reliability to stay connected to the market. Slow or unreliable internet can mean missed opportunities, as even a split-second delay can result in significant losses. Professional day traders often invest in the highest available speed tier or even multiple connections to ensure they never lose connectivity during a critical moment.

Financial Cost of Reliable Internet and Backup Connections

Premium internet plans can cost between $100 and $300 monthly, and some traders also invest in a secondary connection as a backup. This added expense becomes another recurring cost that beginners rarely anticipate, creating an ongoing financial drain.

- **Example: Mark's Missed Win**
  Mark started trading with a standard internet connection, thinking it would suffice. However, during a volatile trading session, his internet lagged just long enough to miss a major sell opportunity, costing him several hundred dollars. Frustrated, he upgraded to a premium plan and added a mobile data backup service, doubling his monthly internet costs. Each monthly payment now reminded him of his

missed opportunity, and he felt trapped in the constant need to cover his overhead.

5. Ergonomic Furniture: An Often Overlooked Necessity for Long-Term Health

The Physical Demands of Day Trading

Day trading requires hours spent sitting in front of multiple monitors, often with intense focus and limited breaks. Poorly designed furniture can lead to physical discomfort, back pain, and long-term health issues. An ergonomic chair and adjustable desk are essential for preventing these issues, allowing traders to maintain focus and productivity without sacrificing physical well-being.

The Steep Cost of Ergonomic Office Equipment

A high-quality ergonomic chair can cost between $500 and $1,000, and sit-stand desks or adjustable desks can add another $400 to $1,000. For beginners with limited capital, these costs may seem excessive, yet the alternative—working without ergonomic support—can lead to long-term health problems that make trading unsustainable.

- **Example: Lisa's Painful Realization**
  Lisa, a new trader eager to build her career, started trading from her kitchen table and chair. Within weeks, she experienced severe back and neck pain. She eventually invested $1,500 in an ergonomic setup, seeing it as a necessary expense. The purchase drained her savings, and she

found herself torn between her physical well-being and financial stress. Each dollar spent on her ergonomic setup weighed on her, and she often felt guilty for needing such an expensive environment just to feel physically capable of trading.

6. Specialized Software and Premium Data Feeds: Expensive but Essential Tools

The Importance of Specialized Tools

Many platforms offer basic tools, but serious day traders often invest in specialized software for charting, real-time data feeds, and algorithmic analysis. These tools provide the insights and analytics needed to make rapid, informed decisions, but they come with significant subscription fees.

High Monthly and Annual Subscription Costs

Advanced trading platforms, premium data feeds, and specialized charting tools often cost $50 to $300 per month. These recurring expenses add up to thousands of dollars each year, and for beginners without steady profits, they become an additional source of pressure and financial stress.

- **Example: Dave's Software Trap**
  Dave started with a $100/month charting tool, but as he progressed, he felt pressured to upgrade to a $250/month plan with more advanced features. His total monthly software expenses grew to over $400, which quickly consumed any profits he made. Each month, he faced the financial reality that his tools were costing him more than he was making,

creating a growing sense of frustration and feeling trapped in a cycle of spending.

7. Ongoing Maintenance and Upgrades: The Never-Ending Expense

The Continuous Need for Equipment Maintenance

Even high-quality equipment needs regular maintenance and occasional repairs, which can interrupt trading sessions and incur additional costs. Computer components can wear out, and software updates often require traders to upgrade their systems, adding unexpected expenses to an already costly setup.

The Expense of Staying Current in a Fast-Paced Industry

Technology evolves quickly, and for traders who rely on their setups daily, the cost of staying current is substantial. Each upgrade or replacement is a reminder of the financial commitment required to maintain a trading station, creating a sense of obligation to continue trading just to justify the expense.

- **Example: Aaron's Relentless Upgrade Cycle**
  Aaron invested in a custom-built trading computer, only to find that software advancements soon outpaced his system's capabilities. He spent $2,000 on upgrades within two years, feeling as though he was caught in a cycle of constant reinvestment. The mounting costs made him question his initial decision, and he felt trapped by the necessity to continually upgrade his system just to keep up.

8. The Psychological Impact of High Overhead Costs

The Weight of Constant Financial Obligations

High overhead costs create a relentless financial pressure for traders, especially those who aren't yet seeing consistent profits. Each subscription fee, equipment upgrade, or internet bill reminds them of the ongoing cost of maintaining their trading setup, creating a mental burden that compounds over time.

The Pressure to Perform and the Emotional Toll

With each month's overhead, traders feel the urgent need to perform well, often taking on riskier trades in hopes of covering their expenses. This pressure can lead to burnout, poor decision-making, and an overwhelming sense of dread when profits fall short of covering costs.

Conclusion: Understanding the Real Cost of a Day Trading Setup

Dispelling the Low-Cost Myth of Day Trading

For those considering day trading, it's essential to see past the minimalist setups presented by influencers. The real cost of professional day trading equipment is substantial, with high upfront costs and ongoing expenses that can quickly consume profits.

Encouraging Thoughtful Financial Planning

Before diving into day trading, you should consider you financial capacity and weigh the ongoing commitment required to maintain a high-performance setup. This reality check can help you avoid the financial and emotional toll that comes with the hidden costs of professional day trading.

Chapter 12:

The Financial Gurus' Web of Deception

1. Introduction: The Allure of "Expert" Guidance in Day Trading

The Desire for Reliable Guidance in a Complex Field

For many, day trading is daunting; the endless streams of data, complex strategies, and high stakes create a steep learning curve. This initial complexity leaves beginners craving a guiding hand, and gurus step in to fill this need. Presenting themselves as seasoned experts, these influencers simplify the process, promising followers a shortcut to financial freedom. Through charismatic presentations and carefully crafted content, they convince followers that with the right guidance, they too can achieve rapid success.

The Rise of Financial "Gurus" and Influencers

Social media's instant reach has transformed these gurus into celebrities in the financial world. Their high-quality videos showcase luxurious lifestyles—mansions, sports cars, and exotic travel locations—portraying day trading as a pathway to such wealth. This luxury imagery taps into the desire for upward mobility, enticing followers who feel trapped by their financial circumstances. Seeing these influencers succeed builds a hopeful belief that anyone can replicate this success by following the guru's "tried-and-true" methods.

2. Investment Portfolios and the Promise of Outsourced Success

Selling Portfolio Management as a Shortcut

The idea of letting an experienced "pro" manage investments on behalf of followers is tempting, especially for beginners who feel unprepared for the risks of trading alone. These gurus frame portfolio management as a shortcut to trading success, emphasizing that followers don't need to worry about complex decision-making—they can simply "sit back" and let the expert work.

False Promises and "Guaranteed" Returns

Unlike legitimate advisors, these gurus make lofty promises of substantial, guaranteed returns with minimal risk. They assure followers that their track record speaks for itself and that followers can expect similar gains by placing their funds in the guru's hands. The assurance of high returns with low fees is designed to win over those looking for "risk-free" gains, even though such promises are unrealistic and highly suspect.

- **Example: Emma's "Expert-Managed" Losses**
  Emma, new to trading, invested $5,000 with a guru promising quarterly returns of 15%. When her portfolio began to lose value, the guru explained that these were "temporary market adjustments" and encouraged her to invest more to "weather the storm." Emma eventually lost 60% of her initial investment, realizing too late that the guru's reassurances were hollow and designed to keep her financially committed.

3. The Myth of Low Fees and "Bank-Busting" Savings

Misleading Claims of Affordable Financial Services

Many influencers claim that they charge far less than banks or traditional financial advisors, framing themselves as affordable, accessible alternatives. They often market themselves as "rebels" who reject the high fees associated with traditional finance, positioning their services as "fair" and more transparent than mainstream advisors.

Hidden Costs and Fine Print

However, these so-called "low fees" often come with hidden charges, like monthly subscription fees, penalties for accessing funds, and even fees for withdrawing from the account. While they promise simplicity and affordability, the guru's income actually relies on a complicated fee structure that followers only discover once they're already financially invested.

- **Case Study: Tony's Deceptive Fee Schedule**
  Tony signed up for a service with a financial influencer who marketed low fees as a key advantage over banks. Within months, Tony discovered numerous hidden fees that chipped away at his profits, including unexpected charges for "market analysis," "exclusive tips," and "investment monitoring." By the end of the year, these fees had totaled over $1,000, far exceeding the original "low-cost" promise.

4. Influencer Marketing and Paid Testimonials: Building a False Sense of Trust

Creating Credibility Through Paid Promotions

Financial influencers often collaborate with popular creators in related fields—lifestyle, personal finance, or fitness influencers—to expand their reach. These creators praise the guru's products or services, presenting a crafted image of widespread success. What followers don't realize is that these partnerships are often purely transactional, with the influencer paying for endorsements and providing prepared scripts.

The Power of Fake Testimonials

The guru may go further, presenting testimonials that are staged or fabricated. They hire actors or repurpose online images, posting these fake testimonials as proof of success. These testimonials manipulate followers into believing that positive results are common, leading them to think they're missing out on guaranteed gains.

- **Example: Lily's Belief in a Staged Success Story**
  Lily found herself captivated by an influencer's "client" who supposedly turned $2,000 into $100,000 in six months. The story seemed genuine, complete with staged screenshots and success testimonials. Trusting the story, Lily invested thousands in the influencer's mentorship program. It wasn't until later that she discovered the "client" was an actor, leaving her feeling betrayed and financially overextended.

5. Affiliate Links and Commission-Driven "Advice"

The Profit Motive Behind "Recommended Tools"

Influencers often promote specific trading platforms, tools, or services as "essential" for success, leading followers to believe that without these products, they won't be able to trade effectively. The guru's profit motive is hidden behind affiliate links, with each purchase bringing in a commission. The financial gains for the guru are substantial, while the followers end up with expensive tools that add little value.

The Hidden Costs of Following "Essential" Recommendations
Many followers believe that investing in these tools will be key to their success, only to find that these products are costly and don't necessarily enhance their performance. Some discover too late that free or lower-cost options would have sufficed for their needs.

- **Example: Josh's Costly Affiliate Trap**
  Josh followed an influencer's advice to sign up for a $300/month data feed, believing it was vital for his trading strategy. After six months, Josh realized he had spent $1,800 on a tool that he barely used, all because the influencer's endorsement implied it was indispensable. Feeling manipulated, Josh was left financially drained and resentful.

6. The Psychological Manipulation of Urgency and FOMO

Creating a Sense of Scarcity and Urgency
Many gurus create artificial scarcity through countdown timers, limited spots, or "special edition" products. These tactics activate the fear of missing out (FOMO), making followers feel they must act immediately or lose out on an exclusive opportunity.

The Emotional Impact of "Act Now" Messages
This manufactured urgency triggers impulse buying, particularly

among those who already feel uncertain or anxious about their financial security. Believing they have a limited time to make a life-changing decision, followers often act before fully evaluating the product or service.

- **Example: Nadia's FOMO-Driven Decision**
  Nadia was struggling financially when an influencer announced a "final chance" mentorship program with only five spots left. Overcome by FOMO, she signed up for the $1,500 program, only to later realize the program was repeatedly offered as a "last chance." Feeling betrayed and financially strained, Nadia's confidence in her financial decisions took a severe hit.

7. The Hidden Trap of Equipment Recommendations

Selling the Dream Through Expensive Equipment

To maintain the illusion of professionalism, influencers often recommend pricey equipment—multi-monitor setups, specialized trading desks, and high-speed computers—as "necessary" for serious trading. These items are promoted as key investments, but the true goal is to profit through affiliate commissions.

Profiting from the Equipment Trap

The guru makes money each time a follower purchases through their link, even though most beginners don't require such high-end setups. These unnecessary expenses drain the follower's funds, adding financial pressure.

- **Example: Michael's Equipment Spiral**
  Michael spent thousands on a top-tier trading station, believing it would increase his chances of success. He soon realized that the expensive setup didn't impact his trading outcomes, leaving him feeling trapped by a costly financial commitment he couldn't justify.

8. The Psychological Toll of Dependency and "False Hope"

Creating a Dependency on Paid Services

Gurus create a cycle of dependency by constantly offering "advanced" tools, updated strategies, or "next-level" courses, implying that success lies just beyond the next purchase. This reinforces a feeling of inadequacy among followers, making them believe that without the guru's guidance, they can't succeed.

The Emotional Cost of False Hope

Followers who don't achieve success are often subtly blamed for not following the program closely enough, encouraging them to buy more services in an attempt to "get it right." This creates a cycle of self-blame and continual spending.

- **Example: Sam's Cycle of Dependency**
  Sam believed each new course and tool from his favorite influencer would finally unlock his success. Each purchase left him no closer to his goals but too financially and emotionally invested to walk away. The cycle left Sam drained, both financially and mentally, as he continued chasing results that never materialized.

Conclusion: Breaking Free from the Guru Trap

Recognizing the Red Flags of Influencer Marketing

By understanding the motives behind these tactics, can ou recognize red flags like promises of guaranteed returns, heavy use of urgency tactics, and affiliate-driven recommendations. Knowledge of these warning signs empowers you to critically evaluate these offers, helping you avoid costly traps.

Encouraging Independent Decision-Making

You should focus on independent learning, relying on affordable or free resources. By fostering critical thinking and self-sufficiency, you can avoid the dependency loop that gurus seek to create. True success in day trading comes from building one's own strategy, learning from mistakes, and resisting the allure of "shortcut" promises.

Chapter 13:

Financial Disaster – When Day Trading Takes Everything

1. Introduction: The Cost of Chasing Dreams

The Irresistible Appeal of Financial Freedom

Day trading captivates the imagination by promising financial freedom, empowerment, and the chance to escape the constraints of traditional work. For many, it represents not just wealth but a new identity—a vision of success unbounded by a 9-to-5 schedule, financial limitations, or outside pressures. The appeal is immediate, powerful, and often highly personal.

Confronting the Disparity Between Dreams and Reality

This chapter doesn't shy away from the sobering truth that for many, the pursuit of day trading dreams ends in financial devastation. It's a journey from optimism to reality, illustrating how the high hopes of success clash with the harsh risks and challenges of day trading. For those who have invested everything only to lose it, this chapter aims to offer empathy, guidance, and a compassionate exploration of the struggles that often go untold.

2. The Trap of Compounding Losses

Chasing Losses: A Dangerous Cycle

The first setback is often brushed aside as a minor inconvenience or a small price to pay for learning. But as losses accumulate, traders enter a vicious cycle of "recouping" their investments. This mindset, driven by a need to validate one's efforts and erase financial pain, intensifies as losses deepen. Each failed attempt to recover leads to greater urgency, and each urgent trade becomes riskier and more irrational, creating a spiral that seems impossible to break.

Psychological and Financial Strain Intensifies with Each Trade
Compounding losses have a psychological effect as well as a financial one. The trader experiences escalating levels of stress, self-blame, and desperation. This internal battle adds pressure with every new trade, driving traders to double down on risky decisions in the hope of a quick turnaround. Instead of finding relief, traders are trapped in a cycle where they are simultaneously trying to fix past losses while creating new ones.

- **Example: Kevin's Downward Spiral**
  Kevin, a retail worker in his 40s, entered day trading with hopes of supplementing his income. After losing $500 in his first month, he increased his trades, each time convinced that "one big win" would recover everything. Within a year, he had lost over $20,000, resorting to payday loans and maxing out credit cards to sustain his trading account. What started as a hopeful side income became a financial pit from which he struggled to escape, affecting his mental health, relationships, and future prospects.

3. Debt Accumulation and Borrowed Funds

From Emergency Funds to Desperation Loans

Once personal savings are exhausted, traders often turn to more extreme measures to maintain their trading. Emergency savings, rainy-day funds, and even retirement accounts become sources of capital, gradually transforming what was once cautious optimism into reckless desperation. Many believe that if they just put in a little more money, they'll finally achieve the success they were promised.

The Compounding Pressure of High-Interest Debt

As personal funds disappear, traders increasingly rely on high-interest credit cards, payday loans, and personal loans. This additional financial strain turns every trade into a high-stakes gamble. The pressure of making monthly payments, compounded by interest, adds an unbearable layer of stress, pushing individuals to take riskier trades in a desperate attempt to escape mounting debt.

- **Case Study: Laura's Debt Cycle**
  Laura, a 32-year-old office manager, initially invested $5,000 from her savings. Following a series of small losses, she borrowed $15,000, convinced that she would eventually break even. Instead, her losses continued, leaving her with a $20,000 debt and a damaged credit score. She was unable to make minimum payments, and the growing financial pressure began affecting her performance at work and her personal relationships. Her trading journey ended in bankruptcy, and her self-esteem took years to recover.

4. The Emotional Toll of Financial Ruin

Feelings of Guilt, Shame, and Despair

Beyond the numbers, financial disaster from day trading leaves deep emotional scars. Those who experience financial ruin often feel an overwhelming sense of guilt and shame. They blame themselves for their losses, questioning their intelligence, discipline, and value as individuals. This self-blame can be crippling, pushing traders into isolation as they fear the judgment of friends and family.

Mental Health Decline and Psychological Effects

The stress and pressure to "fix" financial losses take a severe toll on mental health. Anxiety, insomnia, depression, and even panic attacks become common as traders grapple with the emotional fallout of their losses. The psychological burden of facing financial ruin often goes hand in hand with a loss of self-worth, as the dream of success transforms into a nightmare of financial despair.

- **Example: Mike's Mental Health Decline**

  Mike, a hopeful trader, initially saw day trading as a way to gain control over his finances. But as losses mounted, he experienced constant anxiety and sleepless nights, leading to panic attacks that impacted his daily life. Eventually, he sought therapy to process the overwhelming sense of loss and disappointment, acknowledging that his mental health had been severely impacted by the pursuit of financial freedom.

5. Relationship Damage and Social Isolation

The Erosion of Marital and Family Relationships

Financial strain from day trading affects not only the individual but also their loved ones. As money disappears, so does trust, as partners and family members often feel betrayed by hidden debts or drained savings. Financial losses lead to resentment, blame, and a sense of betrayal, all of which can erode even the strongest relationships.

Social Isolation and Shame-Induced Withdrawal

Many traders withdraw from social circles due to shame, embarrassment, and a desire to avoid questions about their finances. The isolation is compounded by the emotional pain of keeping secrets from loved ones. This loneliness exacerbates the feelings of guilt and self-doubt, as traders spiral further into self-blame and isolation.

- **Case Study: Emily's Family Fallout**

  Emily, a dedicated mother, kept her day trading losses hidden from her husband, hoping to surprise him with financial gains. When he discovered the debts she'd accumulated, he was heartbroken. The couple's relationship became strained, as trust was replaced by resentment and disappointment. Emily's experience highlights the collateral damage day trading can inflict on families, leaving emotional wounds that take years to heal.

6. Loss of Financial Stability and Long-Term Goals

Financial Security Compromised for Day Trading

For many, day trading becomes an all-consuming pursuit, with long-term financial security sacrificed for short-term risk. Emergency funds, college savings, and retirement accounts are drained, leaving traders without a safety net. The realization that their future stability has been compromised is often the hardest pill to swallow.

Sacrificing Major Life Goals

The losses incurred in day trading frequently prevent individuals from achieving major life goals. Those hoping to buy homes, start businesses, or retire early are forced to confront the reality that their decisions have left them with nothing but debt and financial insecurity.

- **Example: David's Shattered Retirement Plans**
  David, nearing retirement, dipped into his savings to fund his trading account, convinced he could recoup his losses. When his account was drained, he faced the painful realization that his retirement plans were destroyed. The setback forced him to continue working years longer than anticipated, shattering his dreams of a peaceful retirement.

7. The Role of Financial Gurus in Exacerbating Disaster

The Allure of Financial Gurus and Their Empty Promises

Financial gurus target vulnerable individuals with promises of quick success and simple strategies. By projecting an image of effortless wealth, they create a false sense of security. Many who follow these gurus do so out of trust and admiration, convinced that these "experts" hold the secrets to financial freedom.

Creating Dependency Through Emotional Manipulation

Gurus often foster dependency by positioning themselves as the gatekeepers to success. They reinforce the idea that consistent investment in their courses, tools, and mentorships is essential. Followers, already financially and emotionally invested, find it hard to walk away, even when results fall short.

- **Case Study: Sarah's Experience with a "Genuine" Guru**
  Sarah trusted a financial guru who promised transparency and honesty. Over time, she invested in every program he offered, convinced each was her key to success. But each new product led only to disappointment and debt. By the time she realized the cycle, she had lost thousands, along with her trust in her own financial judgment.

8. Recovering from Financial Disaster: A Path Forward

Acceptance and Acknowledgment of Losses

The first step to recovery is acknowledging the reality of one's situation. Accepting the losses allows individuals to break free from the shame and guilt that often trap them in isolation. Recognizing that many others have experienced similar struggles can provide comfort and motivation to rebuild.

Seeking Support and Rebuilding Self-Confidence

Financial recovery isn't only about money—it's about regaining self-trust and confidence. Speaking openly with loved ones, friends, or professionals can provide emotional relief. Support networks help ease the burden and remind individuals that they are not alone in their journey to recovery.

Developing Practical Financial Plans for Recovery

Once the emotional groundwork has been laid, practical steps toward financial recovery become essential. Consulting a financial advisor can help individuals create a sustainable plan for managing debt, rebuilding savings, and prioritizing financial stability over short-term gains. This process is gradual, but it is essential for achieving long-term financial health.

Conclusion: Embracing Caution, Self-Compassion, and Resilience

Worst Case Examples could not be shared here as the book's age rating would have to go up.

Most of the stories shared in this book are real-life cases, though names have been changed out of respect for the individuals involved.

Lessons in Caution and Realistic Expectations

The stories in this book serve as reminders to approach day trading—and all high-stakes investments—with caution. Success in trading is not just a matter of skill but of luck, timing, and access to resources. Learning to separate realistic goals from lofty promises is a lesson in self-protection.

The Value of Self-Compassion in Recovery

Compassion for oneself is key to rebuilding after a financial disaster. Recognizing that mistakes do not define one's worth allows individuals to move forward with a sense of dignity and hope, rather than carrying the weight of regret. Self-compassion fosters resilience, enabling individuals to find peace in the process of rebuilding.

A Final Note on Empathy, Resilience, and Growth Beyond Wealth

This chapter honors the strength and resilience of those who have pursued day trading, for their stories of loss also reflect courage, determination, and hope. Day trading's promises may be hollow, but the experiences of those who endure its trials offer invaluable lessons in resilience and perspective. Life's true wealth lies not in financial success but in self-respect, growth, and the resilience to recover from adversity.

Chapter 14:

The Hard Truth — Why Day Trading Isn't for Everyone

By now, it should be evident that day trading is not the easy road to riches that it's often portrayed to be. It is emotionally draining, physically taxing, and financially demanding, and while some individuals might have the resources and support systems to make a genuine attempt, others face significant, often overlooked, barriers that make success much harder—or even impossible. From educational hurdles to life circumstances and hidden disabilities, this chapter sheds light on why day trading, despite what's promised, is not for everyone.

Educational Barriers

Day trading involves a steep learning curve, especially for those without a background in finance or investments. Financial concepts like market analysis, chart reading, and risk management are not inherently simple, and they require a solid foundation in basic financial literacy to grasp effectively. Imagine two individuals: one who has worked in finance, such as a bank teller or financial advisor, versus someone without any formal training or experience in managing money. The latter will need to spend significantly more time and money on self-education—through books, online courses, and training programs—to reach even a beginner's level of comprehension.

For individuals who might struggle with reading or have limited access to reliable resources, the educational demands become even greater. Learning day trading doesn't just involve understanding the markets but also involves interpreting complex data, grasping technical analysis, and, for many, trying to decode the "expert" advice found online. The time and financial investment required to bridge this knowledge gap can be overwhelming, and for those without a strong educational background, this barrier alone can deter any realistic attempt at success.

Physical Limitations

Despite the popular notion that day trading is accessible to anyone with a computer and internet connection, physical abilities can indeed play a critical role. For individuals with severe physical disabilities, working from home may offer flexibility, but it doesn't remove the challenges posed by prolonged sitting, screen time, and high-stakes decision-making. Physical conditions such as chronic pain, limited mobility, or severe fatigue can impact the ability to stay alert, make rapid decisions, and sustain focus for hours at a time.

Even those with milder physical limitations—such as chronic back pain, carpal tunnel syndrome, or reduced stamina—find themselves at a disadvantage. While these conditions might seem manageable, the continuous strain of day trading often exacerbates symptoms. Trading from a home desk doesn't make the task any less demanding; in fact, the solo, isolated nature of day trading can make these physical limitations more pronounced. Simple physical discomfort can escalate into significant obstacles when every moment of focus and clarity counts. Those with physical limitations face a reality that the day trading industry seldom acknowledges—despite the image of accessibility it projects.

Psychological and Mental Health Challenges

Mental resilience is often highlighted as one of the core requirements for day traders, and for good reason. The rapid pace of the markets, the financial pressure, and the highs and lows of profit and loss are emotionally intense. However, for individuals with psychological or mental health conditions, these pressures are far more challenging. Day trading demands a unique combination of focus, emotional control, and stress management that may simply be incompatible with certain mental health conditions.

For example, individuals with moderate to severe depression, anxiety, or attention-deficit disorders might struggle significantly in this field. Each trade requires quick decisions, often under pressure, and every loss has the potential to amplify negative emotions. While some traders are equipped to handle the inherent stress, those with pre-existing mental health conditions are more vulnerable to emotional burnout and decision fatigue.

Adding to this challenge are "hidden" or unrecognized disabilities—conditions that may not meet clinical thresholds for diagnosis but still impact day-to-day functioning. These low-level psychological or cognitive disabilities can quietly undermine a trader's performance without their knowledge. Studies suggest that millions of individuals fall into this category, experiencing symptoms of mild depression, chronic stress, or anxiety without ever receiving formal diagnosis or support. Yet these challenges affect areas critical to day trading, such as decision-making, emotional regulation, and resilience under pressure. For individuals who unknowingly fall into this category, day trading can prove to be an insurmountable challenge without support or awareness.

Life Circumstances: Single Parents and Caregivers

Single parents and caregivers, while often encouraged by promises of financial freedom, face significant hurdles in day trading that aren't typically acknowledged. Day trading requires constant attention to the markets, readiness to respond instantly to changes, and the capacity to handle prolonged screen time—all of which are incredibly difficult to manage when raising a family solo. Single parents, who juggle the demands of parenting, work, and personal obligations, often find themselves distracted or exhausted, making it nearly impossible to maintain the steady focus that day trading requires.

Likewise, caregivers for family members with special needs or health conditions face similar challenges. For many caregivers, day trading represents a potential way to work from home while fulfilling their responsibilities. However, the unpredictability of caregiving tasks—ranging from medical emergencies to constant attention—interferes with the structured, consistent approach needed to succeed in day trading. Family obligations rarely align with market hours, and every moment away from the screen can mean a missed opportunity or increased risk.

These individuals are often sold the same "you can succeed if you work hard enough" message, ignoring the specific constraints they face. For many single parents and caregivers, day trading is simply incompatible with their daily lives, despite the promises made by day trading advocates.

People with High-Stress or Time-Consuming Jobs

A popular pitch among day trading influencers is that anyone in a stressful or low-paying job can break free by becoming a day trader. However, many people with high-stress or demanding jobs find that day trading adds to, rather than alleviates, their existing pressures. Day trading requires a considerable amount of energy, focus, and emotional stamina, and for someone already exhausted from a high-stress job, maintaining these qualities is challenging.

Imagine someone who works long hours in healthcare, retail, or hospitality—a field with unpredictable hours or a heavy workload—attempting to day trade after work. Fatigue, distraction, and the pressure to make quick, important decisions do not mix well. For those already managing a demanding job, day trading often leads to burnout rather than the financial freedom promised.

Financial Constraints and Responsibility Burdens

Day trading is, at its core, a financial commitment. It requires disposable income for trading capital, platform fees, and ongoing education. For individuals with limited financial resources, minimal disposable income, or personal debt, day trading creates additional stress and risk. The pressure to succeed, combined with a lack of financial cushion, often leads individuals to make desperate or impulsive decisions in the hopes of "catching up" or recouping losses.

Individuals supporting family members, living paycheck to paycheck, or managing high monthly expenses don't have the luxury of taking the calculated, patient approach that successful day trading demands. For those without a strong financial foundation, day trading is a high-risk endeavor that can worsen financial strain rather than alleviate it. Single-income households, particularly those with dependents, face these pressures acutely, often leading to outcomes far different from what day trading ads promise.

The Misleading Promise of "If You Just Work Hard Enough"

Despite these significant obstacles, a powerful narrative persists: that success in day trading is a matter of hard work and persistence. The popular message—perpetuated by influencers, government initiatives, and some trading platforms—is that anyone can succeed if they are dedicated enough. But in truth, hard work alone does not erase the structural, physical, and financial barriers that make day trading unrealistic for many.

The reality is that day trading success is not evenly accessible. Personal circumstances, limitations, and responsibilities vary widely, and hard work alone does not compensate for the absence of financial stability, physical wellness, or mental resilience. For those with added barriers—whether due to physical, educational, psychological, or life circumstances—day trading's promise of universal success is misleading and, in some cases, harmful. Recognizing these obstacles is essential for anyone considering this path, especially given the high risks and costs involved.

Conclusion: Facing the Truth and Setting Realistic Expectations

As this book has shown, day trading is far from the universal "get rich quick" solution it's often made out to be. Success in this field requires more than just effort; it demands a solid foundation of financial, physical, and emotional resources that not everyone possesses. The promise that "anyone can succeed" in day trading disregards the realities of those with distinct disadvantages. Instead of blindly following the dream, potential traders need to realistically assess their personal circumstances and resources before embarking on a path that often leads to more loss than gain.

By understanding the barriers detailed in this chapter, you can make more informed decisions about whether day trading is genuinely a viable path for you, or if the promise of success is simply another of the many "lies" sold by day trading's public image.

Final Words

You don't have to abandon your dream of day trading or working from home, but now you've been warned: this is a journey, not a sprint, and one that comes with numerous hidden costs. For some, it may be wise to consider professional help and rely on a licensed financial advisor from a reputable institution to manage their finances.

Further Reading for the Aspiring Day Trader

Book Recommendation

If you're interested in building a solid foundation for day trading, gaining a deeper understanding of advanced strategies, and exploring professional-level tactics, consider these titles by Cornelius Nathaniel Goldman. Each book is crafted to guide readers through the complexities of day trading, offering clear insights for every stage of your trading journey.

1. **Day Trading for Beginners: Key Tips**
   Get Started with Confidence
   Perfect for newcomers, this introductory guide simplifies the fundamentals of day trading, breaking down essential techniques and strategies to help you navigate the markets with clarity. *Day Trading for Beginners* covers everything you need to know to make informed trades, from understanding market trends to developing a mindset for success.

2. **Advanced Day Trading: Mastering Risk and Profitability**
   Elevate Your Trading Skills
   For traders looking to take their skills to the next level, this advanced guide explores the nuances of managing risk, maximizing profitability, and adapting to changing market conditions. *Advanced Day Trading* dives deep into sophisticated strategies and provides actionable advice for experienced traders aiming to hone their abilities and achieve consistent results.

3. **Day Trading for Professionals: Master-Level Strategies for Consistent Profits**

Become a Master of the Trade

Designed for seasoned traders, this professional-level manual covers high-level strategies to help you sustain consistent profits. *Day Trading for Professionals* reveals insights into mastering complex techniques, from multi-market trading and options to algorithmic strategies and advanced risk assessment. This guide is essential for those committed to achieving mastery in day trading.

Legal Disclaimer

The information provided in *Day Trading Lies* is for informational purposes only and reflects the personal opinions and experiences of the author, Cornelius Nathaniel Goldman. This book is not intended to provide financial, investment, legal, or other professional advice. Readers should consult qualified professionals regarding any financial or investment decisions.

The author and publisher have made every effort to ensure the accuracy of the information within this book as of the publication date. However, they assume no responsibility for errors, omissions, or any outcomes from the use of this information. Any reliance readers place on such information is strictly at their own risk.

Any references to specific individuals, content creators, financial experts, or so-called "gurus" are based on general industry practices and behaviors, not on specific individuals, businesses, or entities, unless expressly stated otherwise. The author does not endorse any third-party products, services, or companies, and any similarity to actual persons, living or dead, or actual events is purely coincidental.

This book critiques practices within the financial industry as a whole and is not intended to harm the reputation or business of any individual or organization. It aims to provide readers with an understanding of the risks associated with day trading and the importance of informed decision-making.

By reading this book, readers agree that the author and publisher will not be liable for any loss or damages—direct, indirect, incidental, or consequential—arising from the information within this book or from any reliance on it.